THE
GREAT WAR
ILLUSTRATED
1916

THE GREAT WAR ILLUSTRATED

1916

A selection of 1,300 images illustrating events at Kut-al-Amara, Verdun, Jutland and the Somme

William Langford & Jack Holroyd

Pen & Sword
MILITARY

Dedicated to the One True Sovereign
who was disregarded by the nations when, in 1914, men elected to fight
among themselves on behalf of their own sovereignties

First published in Great Britain in 2016 by
PEN & SWORD MILITARY
an imprint of
Pen & Sword Books Ltd,
47 Church Street, Barnsley,
South Yorkshire.
S70 2AS

Copyright © William Langford & Jack Holroyd 2016

ISBN 978 1 47388 157 0

The right of William Langford & Jack Holroyd to be identified as Authors of this Work
has been asserted by them in accordance with the
Copyright, Designs and Patents Act 1988.

A CIP catalogue record for this book is available
from the British Library

Designed by Factionpress
Printed and bound in India by Replika Press Pvt. Ltd.

Pen & Sword Books Ltd incorporates the imprints of
Pen & Sword Aviation, Pen & Sword Maritime,
Pen & Sword Military, Pen & Sword Select, Pen & Sword Military Classics,
Leo Cooper, Wharncliffe Local History

For a complete list of Pen & Sword titles please contact:
PEN & SWORD BOOKS LIMITED
47 Church Street, Barnsley, South Yorkshire, S70 2AS, England.
E-mail: enquiries@pen-and-sword.co.uk
Website: www.pen-and-sword.co.uk

Contents

Foreword

by Nigel Cave

The Great War Illustrated 1916

This is the third volume of photographs and commentary that have been published by Pen & Sword in the last couple of years, a fitting tribute to the photographers of the Great War. A feature of the books is the coloured photography section. Although this has been made a far easier process because of the possibilities of digital manipulation, it requires considerable skill and extensive knowledge of the equipment and conditions of the time to make such work as realistic as possible.

In a book such as this, photographs have to be given context; the solution that has been adapted in the series is to place them in chapters – either relating to a particular event, such as an offensive, or of an emerging theme – in this case the development and mass production of weapons of destruction. This approach allows for a commentary, aided by maps, which provides sufficient information to make sense of what is being portrayed.

1916 was the mid year of the war; when it began the war was sixteen months old and when it ended it still had twenty three to go. 1915 had been, on balance, a good year for the Central Powers – the allies had been ejected from Gallipoli, large numbers of their soldiers were sitting in Salonika, in Greece, unable to develop the war against Bulgaria; there were no signs of any progress at all by the allies on the major fronts in France and Belgium and in Russia. The biggest setback for the central powers had been the entry of Italy, an erstwhile ally of Germany and Austria-Hungary, into the war on the allied side.

Two battles dominated on the Western Front. The most significant in its long term impact was the protracted struggle at Verdun, which lasted from the end of February to the end of December; the bloodiest battle of the war, the Somme, lasted four and a half months and ground mercilessly on through the summer and autumn, culminating in miserable weather conditions in November and a form of stalemate in the mud.

However, there were events elsewhere than on the Western Front. The Mesopotamia campaign, an Indian army affair, started promisingly and then came to a dismal, if temporary, halt at the siege and subsequent surrender of Kut, along with its garrison of 12,000 or so men. In the great scheme of things and in the light of casualty lists elsewhere, this was not particularly significant; however, failure against the Ottoman Turks came all too swiftly on the heels of the abandonment of the Gallipoli campaign by the allies, in January 1916: the score card against the Turks was not looking good. A further notable feature of the surrender of Kut was the abysmal treatment of the prisoners, with a quite horrendous fatality rate; a minority survived the war and the whole affair was a precursor to the treatment of prisoners by the Japanese in the Second World War.

Verdun was a battle whose legacy has been seared onto the collective memory of the French nation, elevating it to myth status. One of the reasons for this was the policy of the rotation of divisions that was adopted by the French commander for much of the battle, General Pétain. This ensured that a very high proportion of the French army experienced the battle and the quite dreadful conditions in which it was fought: if you read no other book on the battle I would recommend Christina Holstein's *Verdun: The Left Bank* (Pen & Sword, 2016). It is a tale of remarkable heroism by both sides, the only light in what makes for dismal reading. The experience of the French at Verdun goes a long way to explaining the Maginot mentality of the inter war years. Indeed, its reach has gone further than that: to understand the Franco-German axis in modern European politics one needs to understand the long lasting impact of this battle.

The Somme 1916 has, of course, a special place in British memory. It is the battle where the hopes and anticipation of a nation were dashed: the all-volunteer (at least at its outset) army of the best of British youth was ground down by a ruthless and experienced foe as an amateur army was transformed into a continental one, ending the battle on equivalent terms with its French and German counterparts. In France the battle has limited recognition, despite the fact that she, too, suffered very heavy casualties – some 200,000 of them. Britain fought more expensive battles when one looks at the daily rate of casualties during the battle – the two intensive periods of fighting in 1918 had a higher rate, as did the spring 1917 Battle of Arras. But for Britain it is 1 July that has left its mark and to a large extent determined the popular perception of the whole war.. The battle also marked the first major intervention on the Western Front by the British dominions. The Canadian division had played a notable part in the Second Battle of Ypres in 1915; by the end of the Somme all (by now four of them) of its divisions had participated in the fighting on the Somme. The Australians, some having already fought a hard campaign in Gallipoli, had three of its five divisions employed on the Somme, whilst one took part in a disastrous attack in French Flanders, at Fromelles, with the aim of pinning the German troops there to that part of the front. New Zealand's division played its full part at the Battle of Flers-Courcelette in September; the South African Brigade is forever associated with Delville Wood; whilst the tiny population of Newfoundland saw its single battalion on the front seemingly all but eliminated at Beaumont Hamel.

The naval war is rarely studied to the same extent as the land war. There are various reasons for this, but one of the most obvious is that there were very few major naval battles: indeed there was only one major surface battle and the long drawn out submarine campaign that dominated naval thinking and strategy, particularly in 1917. Jutland was the biggest naval battle in history. In some respects it was a German victory, if one considers casualties inflicted and tonnage sunk; amongst other things it revealed a weakness in British ship design. However, at the end of the day it was a British strategic victory: the German High Seas Fleet never ventured out of harbour for the rest of the war.

A feature of 1916, from the British perspective, was the mobilisation of Britain's industries to provide the munitions and materiel required to sustain a huge land army and to enable it to fight on equal terms. Shortages of suitable artillery pieces and munitions – both in number and reliability – had plagued the relatively small scale offensives in which the British had been involved in 1915. Even by July 1916 the impact of improved production (for which due credit must be given to David Lloyd George) was yet to be felt: the British were far better equipped by the late autumn than they had been at the beginning of the offensive.

A picture can be worth a thousand words: this photographic record of the events and developments above helps us in our understanding of them – the horrors and the conditions in which these men fought and the effect that these would have on countless women and children and communities who saw the torn and damaged wrecks of humanity who were evacuated home. Women became essential elements in the war machine – whether it be as nurses, as replacements for men in relatively 'safe' military jobs and, increasingly, as munitions workers. Their presence and contribution in these areas was to become ever more obvious as 1916 gave way to 1917.

Of course the photographs do not give us a complete picture – we do not have the sounds, the smells of battlefields and of the dead and wounded, nor of the sense of fear, of comradeship, of resolution; but without them our understanding of the war and of the men who fought it would be considerably more limited. This book provides a fascinating *vade mecum* to the campaigns of 1916.

The Taylor Picture Library

Along with the thousands of photographic prints wartime agencies released to newspapers and later collected by Peter Taylor, there were also many volumes of books printed and that were published during the first quarter of the Twentieth Century. Advancing technology has meant that the printed illustrations contained on their pages can be scanned and corrected to an acceptable standard for reproduction in printed books once more.

They are now over one hundred years old and copyright issues have ceased to be a problem (despite optimistic claims to ownership of images by some).

Collections of magazines printed in the 1920s and 30s have likewise presented a useful source of illustrations for writers, researchers and television production companies.

Images which have previously appeared on the printed pages of magazines and books bear a screen on them which can cause an unsightly pattern when copied and reproduced; however, nowadays the development of computer photographic correcting programmes that can deal with this are available. In skilled hands even black and white photographs can be corrected and coloured to a high standard, although, there are those who would prefer not to employ photographs adulterated in this way.

Of all the various picture-rich magazines sold either weekly or monthly to the British public during the war years, the *Sphere* magazine was ahead of its contemporaries in the quality of paper and size of printed pictures. Today, individual copies of *Sphere* can sell at a premium as designers have become aware of the quality of its printed pictures.

This illustrated series covering the Great War is a selection from the thousands of historic images available; the pictures have been corrected to a standard that a printer of books can work with and these volumes are a convenient catalogue of what is now available from Pen & Sword History Books, based at Barnsley in South Yorkshire.

Chapter One: **British Humiliation at Kut**

16GW401 Turkish machine gunners in a hastily constructed Maxim position in the vicinity of Ctesiphon, eighteen miles from Baghdad.

16GW400 Captured Turkish Maxim machine guns undergoing examination, cleaning and repair by British Army armourers.

16GW402 Following Turkey's entry into the war in November 1914, British strategy, outside Europe focused on the Turkish Empire. By 1915 Turkey was surrounded by enemies intent on her defeat.

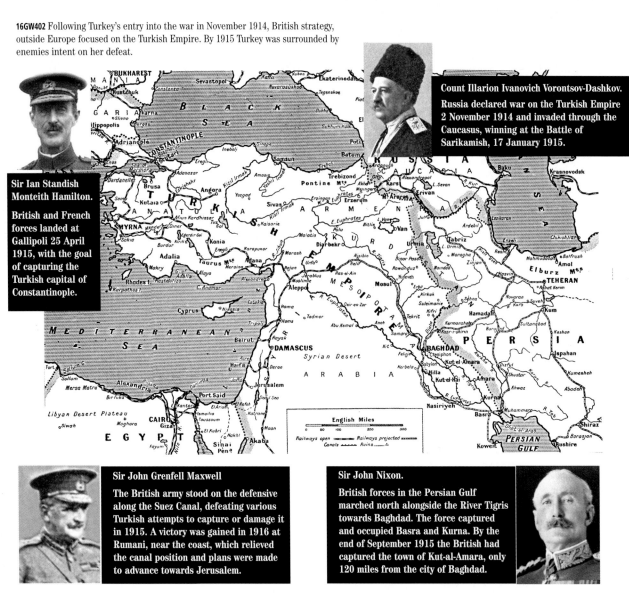

Count Illarion Ivanovich Vorontsov-Dashkov. Russia declared war on the Turkish Empire 2 November 1914 and invaded through the Caucasus, winning at the Battle of Sarikamish, 17 January 1915.

Sir Ian Standish Monteith Hamilton.

British and French forces landed at Gallipoli 25 April 1915, with the goal of capturing the Turkish capital of Constantinople.

Sir John Grenfell Maxwell

The British army stood on the defensive along the Suez Canal, defeating various Turkish attempts to capture or damage it in 1915. A victory was gained in 1916 at Rumani, near the coast, which relieved the canal position and plans were made to advance towards Jerusalem.

Sir John Nixon.

British forces in the Persian Gulf marched north alongside the River Tigris towards Baghdad. The force captured and occupied Basra and Kurna. By the end of September 1915 the British had captured the town of Kut-al-Amara, only 120 miles from the city of Baghdad.

When Turkey joined the world war on the side of the Central Powers of Germany and Austria-Hungary, the British War Cabinet ordered the invasion of Ottoman controlled territories in Mesopotamia (present-day Iraq). British forces in the Persian Gulf, there to protect oil interests at Abadan, marched north alongside the River Tigris towards Baghdad. Against weak Turkish opposition, the force captured and occupied Basra and Kurna. By the end of September 1915 the British 6th Indian Division, commanded by General Charles Townshend, had captured the town of Kut-al-Amara, only 120 miles from Baghdad. Up to that point British casualties had been light, with just sixty-five men killed, whereas 3,000 Turks had surrendered.

However, the situation changed dramatically when the British ran into defensive positions either side of the Tigris at Ctesiphon on 22 November 1915. Over four days a battle raged and, despite heavy casualties, the Turks led by General Yusef Nur-ed-Din defeated the British. More than half of the British force which fought at Ctesiphon (8,500 men) were either killed or wounded. The survivors then endured an agonizing retreat to Kut-al-Amara without adequate medical attention or transport.

16GW425 Leaders of the expedition against the Turkish held city of Baghdad: General Sir John Nixon with his staff officers. Original caption: *After capturing Kut-al-Amara at the end of September* [1915]*, General Nixon's force was some 120 miles from Baghdad by road. On 16 November Reuters reported that they had reached Azizie, within fifty miles of the city, and there have been rumours of advances still nearer Baghdad. Sir John Nixon recently issued a letter to neighbouring Arab sheikhs to deny false reports of the enemy, and to assure them of good treatment. 'The British forces,' he stated, 'after defeating the Turkish forces entrenched at Sinn, have occupied Kut-al-Amara, and are now following the defeated Turkish army up the Tigris.' Mr Asquith said of Sir John Nixon's expedition that 'there had not been, in the whole course of the war, a series of operations more carefully contrived, and more brilliantly conducted.'*

16GW460 Herbert Henry Asquith, Prime Minister of the United Kingdom from 1908 to December 1916.

16GW407a British operations in Mesopotamia, from November 1914 to November 1915; advancing north from Basra, along the course of the River Tigris, with Baghdad as the military goal. (Kut-al-Amara has been circled.)

16GW411 Preparing a marking bouy for placing on the River Tigris.

16GW413 With the British in Mesopotamia. The first Government ice factory to be erected in Basra. Arabian engineers and coolies at work under the direction of the Royal Engineers. This was to supply ice for the hospital.

16GW463 Pumping water from the River Tigris into portable containers.

16GW464a, 16GW482 Indian troops of the 6th (Poona) Division using mules to transport supplies from the harbour to various camps.

In April 1915, the Turks mounted an attack on 7,000 British and Indian troops at Shaiba, southwest of Basra, with a force of 4,000 Turks and 14,000 Arab tribesmen. Against numerical superiority, the Anglo-Indian force inflicted a decisive defeat on the Turks, which ended the threat to Basra. This success caused the British to judge the Turkish soldier to be inferior, which in turn gave rise to a dangerous degree of over confidence. The ground was thus prepared for the disaster at Kut in 1916.

16GW412 A very young Turkish captive.

16GW424 Indian artillery at Shaiba; the weapons are portable mountain guns .

16GW494 Turkish prisoners shortly after capture.

16GW493 Turkish prisoners, quartered in a barrack block, paraded for roll call.

16GW495 Turkish prisoners' food preparation – bread baking facilities.

16GW499 British Army NCOs bartering with the Arabs on the riverside jetty.

16GW497 Arabs captured fighting with the Turks.

16GW498 The prisoners' tobacco ration has arrived and is being distributed to Turkish prisoners.

16GW496 Turkish prison orderlies about to serve out the daily bread ration.

16GW477 Arabs unloading supplies from their river transports.

16GW466 British salvage detail sorting through spent ammunition shell cases.

16GW481 Men of an Indian cavalry brigade before the drive north towards Baghdad.

16GW462 An Indian regimental baggage train.

16GW469 Religious observances adhered to by the nations to beg favour and success over the enemy.

16GW479 A Military Policeman helping a blind beggar.

16GW480 Men from an Indian company awaiting orders; note the Red Cross on the boat.

16GW408a General Townshend and his staff at Kut in September 1915, before the advance to Ctesiphon. Left to right: Captain Clifton (Aide-de-camp to Townshend); Major Forbes (Deputy Assistant Director Transport); Colonel Annesley (Assistant Director Services &Transport); Colonel Evans (General Staff Officer 1); Colonel Hehir (Assistant Director Medical Services); Major General Townshend (General Officer Commanding); Captain Gilchrist (Divisional Artillery and Quartermaster General); Colonel Chitty (Assistant Adjutant and Quartermaster General); Lieutenant Colonel Maude (Commanding Artillery); Lieutenant Colonel Parr; Lieutenant Colonel Wilson (Deputy Commander Royal Engineers).

16GW467 Major General Sir Charles Vere Ferrers Townshend KBC, DSO. The officer who led the ultimately disastrous first British Expedition against Baghdad in the autumn of 1915.

16GW426 General Townshend with two of his staff and escort.

The Siege of Kut-al-Amara

Reinforced by 30,000 troops, the Turks bottled up the British invaders at Kut-al-Amara and there followed a siege which lasted five months. Finally, the half starved garrison of 11,800 British and Indian soldiers surrendered on 29 April 1916. During the siege, conditions for the men in Kut degenerated and, with meagre medical facilities along with bitterly cold weather, many did not survive the winter. All attempts by the British to relieve the trapped force ended in failure.

Major General Sir Charles Townshend

6th (Poona) Infantry Division of the Indian Army

16 (Poona) Brigade

2nd Bn. Dorsetshire Regiment
1st Bn. 20th Duke of Cambridge's Own
Infantry (Brownlow's Punjabis)
1st Bn. 104th Wellesley's Rifles
1st Bn. 117th Mahrattas

17 (Ahmednagar) Brigade

1st Bn. Ox & Bucks
1st Bn. 119th Infantry (The Mooltan
Regiment)
1st Bn. 103rd Mahratta Light Infantry
1st Bn. 22nd Punjabis

18 (Belguam) Brigade

2nd Bn. Norfolk Regiment
1st Bn. 110th Mahratta Light Infantry
1st Bn. 120th Rajputana Infantry
1st Bn. 7th (Duke of Connaught's
Own) Rajputs

Divisional troops
33rd Queen Victoria's Own Light Cavalry
17 Co. 3rd Sappers and Miners
22 Co. 3rd Sappers and Miners
48th Pioneers

Divisional Artillery
X Brigade, Royal Field Artillery (RFA)
76 Bty. RFA
82 Bty. RFA
63 Bty. RFA

1st Indian Mountain Artillery Brigade
23rd (Peshawar) Mountain Battery (Frontier Force)
30th Mountain Battery
1/5th Hampshire Howitzer Battery

16GW468 Inspection of Indian troops.
16GW478 British troops leaving Basra for the march north.

16GW423 Pack mules about to be unloaded after arriving at Shaiba. British artillery can be seen in the background.

16GW492 The Anglo Indian forces preparing to advance on Baghdad: horses loaded on a barge on the River Tigris about to sail.

16GW500 Arab coolies loading a barge under the supervision of British officers.

16GW502 Backing a motor lorry on to dry land from a barge on the Tigris.

16GW503 Landing a lorry for use with the Army Service Corps.

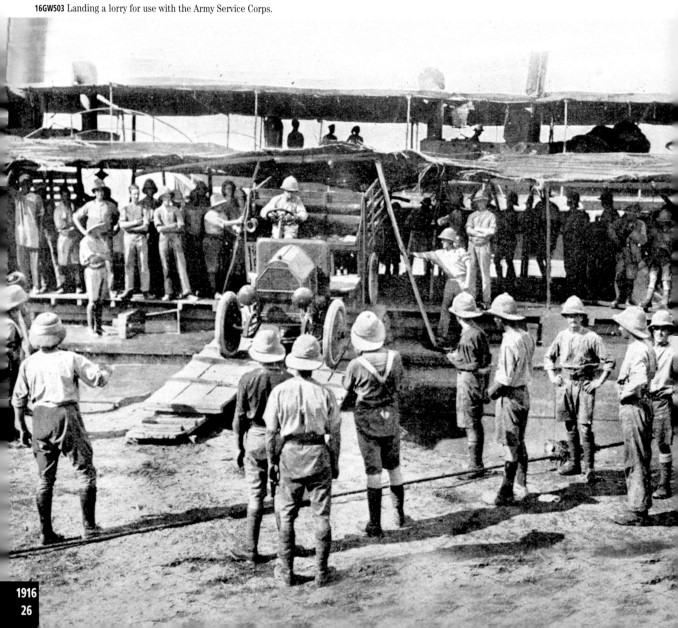

16GW501 British/Indian convoy of trucks taking water from the Tigris.

16GW443 Infantry disembarking from a gunboat on the Tigris during the campaign to capture Baghdad.

16GW422 Indian cavalry crossing an area of flooded desert between Basra and Shaiba.

16GW504 Indian infantry marching through miles of flooded desert.

16GW428 Dorsets marching nine miles across a flooded desert.

16GW404a On the long march, in torrid heat, towards the strategic goal of the Turkish held city of Baghdad.

16GW405a British machine gun section and infantry crossing the River Tigris on a pontoon bridge.

16GW487, 16GW486 A British officer's 'houseboat' (Transport headquarters) on the Tigris. Original Captions: There are on earth fewer hotter places – if any – than Lower Mesopotamia between May and August. The crate on the roof is a hen coop to provide the 'Murgi-roast' (roast fowl), the Indian mess khansamah's staple dish.

16GW490 A crowded transport on the Tigris during the campaign to capture Baghdad.

16GW437 The 2nd Battalion, Dorsetshire Regiment, 16 Brigade, 6th (Poona) Division, on its way up the Tigris, sustained by river boats.

16GW488 Indian troops on a river boat on the Tigris clean their Short Lee Enfield rifles.

16GW489 The British fleet of Fly Class river boats sailing north during the campaign to capture and occupy Baghdad.

16GW450 Brirsh sea planes operating in the Persian Gulf housed on a barge.

16GW420 Armoured car, one of many used by the British Army for patrol work.

16GW515 British soldiers during the advance to Baghdad.

16GW444 Crossing the Tigris in a native boat.

16GW410 British infantry in camp during the march on Baghdad.

16GW465 Abandoned Turkish positions alongside of the Tigris. Earlier successes by the British/Indian force, along with signs of a Turkish retreat to Baghdad, served to convince the British High Command that the Turks had little fighting ability. Thus the scene was set for the coming humiliating defeat at Kut.

16GW427 Ruins of the palace in the city of Ctesiphon, the ancient capitol of the Parthian and Sasanian empires. It was here that the (Indian) 6th Division advancing on Baghdad was stopped and defeated by the Turks in November 1915. The British retreated to Kut-al-Amara, where General Townshend ordered his division to stand and fight.

16GW511 Turkish baggage train on the road.

16GW512 Field Marshal Colmar von der Goltz. German commander of the Ottoman Fifth Army at the Battle of Ctesiphon. After three days fighting both British and Turks withdrew from the battlefield. However, with the British retreating, Goltz turned his army around and followed them down river. When Townshend halted at Kut, Goltz laid siege to the British position. He died from typhus in Baghdad, 19 April 1916, two weeks before the British surrendered at Kut.

16GW419 Victors at the Battle of Ctesiphon, Turkish troops trap the entire Indian 6th (Poona) Division at Kut.

General Townshend was obliged to retire before superior forces, with casualties amounting to approximately one third of the force with which he entered the battle. Over 3,500 wounded had to be removed from the battlefield to the river bank, in some cases a distance of ten miles. A large proportion had to make their way on foot in spite of their injuries. At the river the wounded men were crowded into steamers and barges without proper medical attention. Some of the more fortunate wounded were disembarked at Amarah. The majority went down river to Basra, a journey which, in some cases, took two weeks. The many cases of dysentery aggravated conditions for the wounded on board.

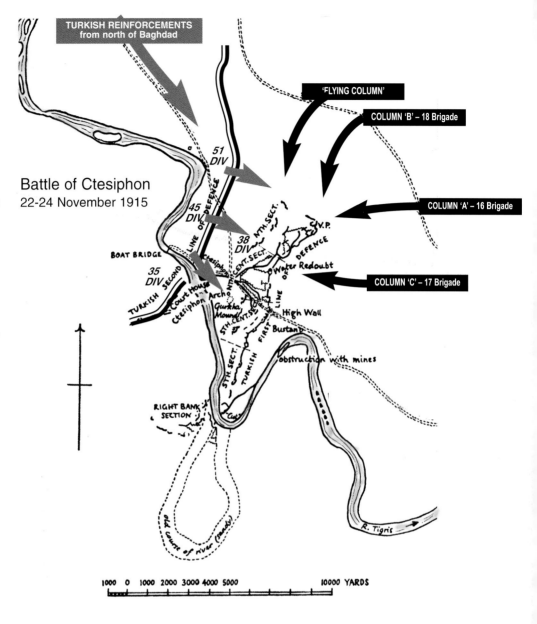

Battle of Ctesiphon
22-24 November 1915

TURKISH REINFORCEMENTS
from north of Baghdad

'FLYING COLUMN'

COLUMN 'B' – 18 Brigade

COLUMN 'A' – 16 Brigade

COLUMN 'C' – 17 Brigade

51 DIV

45 DIV

38 DIV

35 DIV

BOAT BRIDGE

LINE OF DEFENCE

TURKISH SECOND

NTH. SECT.

INT. CENT. SECT.

Court House

Ctesiphon Arch

Gurkha Mound

STH. CENT. SECT.

TURKISH FIRST LINE

S.V.P.

LINE OF DEFENCE

Water Redoubt

High Wall

Bustan

obstruction with mines

STH. SECT.

RIGHT BANK SECTION

old course of river (sandy)

R. Tigris

1000 0 1000 2000 3000 4000 5000   10000 YARDS

16GW509 Defeated by the Turks at Ctesiphon, the Indian 6th Division retreated to Kut, November 1915; this is an 18-pounder field gun team moving at speed.

16GW505 British/Indian cavalry at Ctesiphon in 1915.

16GW516 Cavalry withdrawing to Kut-al-Amara. General Townshend ordered the cavalry to continue back to Basra and consequently it was not bottled up at Kut along with the 6th Division.

16GW525 A steamer arrives at Kut-al-Amara loaded with troops and supplies from the withdrawal following the Battle of Ctesiphon.

16GW526, 16GW527 Men of the 6th Division man-handling an 18-pdr field gun after landing it from a boat on the Tigris at Kut.

16GW529 A British infantry platoon preparing to march out to man the defence perimeter at Kut-al-Amara.

16GW530 A Turkish artillery column marching to Kut to reinforce the divisions besieging Townshend's Anglo-Indian force.

16GW429 Kut-al-Amara, situated on a loop in the River Tigris, was occupied by the 6th (Poona) Division following the Battle of Ctesiphon. General Townhsend decided to hold the town until reinforcements arrived from Basra.

16GW430 A British officer at Kut oversees the unloading of donkeys bearing supplies.

16GW432 The main street of Kut at the time of the seige. The garrison and inhabitants would soon be short of food, as the Turkish army successfully prevented supplies getting through via the river Tigris.

16GW513 A view over the rooftops of Kut during the siege.

16GW517 Norfolk House at Kut-al-Amara, which served as British Headquarters during the seige. Note the wireless mast.

16GW438 British artillery spotter and ranging mast.

16GW518 General Sir Charles Townshend had decided to try and withstand a siege at Kut-al-Amara. A general sense of complacency in fighting the Turks was serving to deliver the British into a situation of acute embarrassment and danger. Townshend organized a defensive perimeter and waited for relief, keeping in mind of what had occured in the famous Relief of Mafeking, fifteen years earlier, in the Boer War.

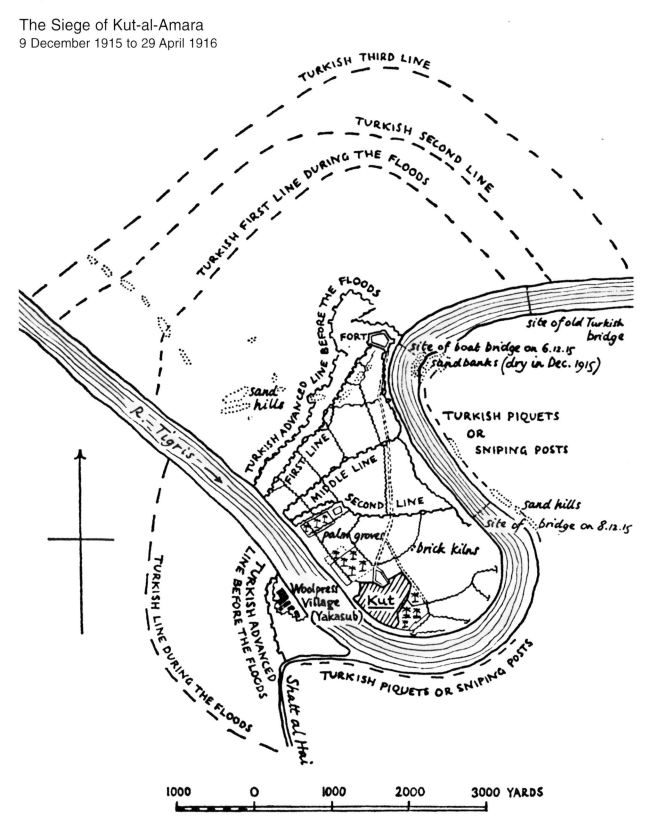

The Siege of Kut-al-Amara
9 December 1915 to 29 April 1916

The 6th (Indian) Division was trapped in this curve of the River Tigris for five months.

16GW470 A Turkish field gun battery in action with Krupp built 77 mm guns.

16GW417 Another enemy of the soldiers of all sides during wartime – lice. Here British soldiers are busy finding and destroying 'chats' from their army blankets.

16GW510 Officers of the 2nd Dorsets in trenches at Kut, surrounded by a Turkish army. Standing is Major Brown, in charge of battalion supplies.

16GW448 Communicating on a field telephone during the siege.

16GW447 Indian infantry-men fitting primers to Mills bombs.

16GW439 An Indian cavalryman demonstrates how to throw a Mills hand-grenade from a trench.

16GW446 A Gurkha operating a Lewis machine gun, firing short bursts at the Turkish positions..

16GW555 Machine gunners of the 48th Pioneers in action against the Turks.

1916
49

16GW506 British infantry Maxim crew in a defensive position.

16GW515 British infantry moving into trenches.

16GW491 British infantry moving through the trenches on the Kut perimeter.

16GW445 British gunners on the Kut perimeter.

16GW520 A casualty being brought into the town – Townshend's HQ can be seen in the background.

16GW519 The British Military Cemetery at Kut. Shells can be seen bursting in the distance during the siege.

16GW435 British graves at Kut.

16GW521 The 4th Field Ambulance HQ, with men gathered for sick parade.

16GW522 Indian Maxim machine gun teams resiting their weapons under the direction of a British officer.

16GW535 Turkish reinforcements being brought down river from Baghdad. The Crescent flag flies in the stern of the specially constructed rafts.

16GW532 Turkish standard bearer and escort at Kut.

16GW523 A truce arranged at Sunnaiyat on the Tigris to exchange prisoners. British and Turkish officers meet in No Man's Land.

16GW524 Turkish officer prisoners captured during the fighting and under Indian guard.

16GW533 Turkish infantry attacking the British defensive perimeter during the siege of Kut.

16GW536 The Commander in Chief in Mesopotamia and his staff: Lieutenant General Sir Percy Lake at GHQ, Basra; General Lake (seated fourth from the right) succeeded General Sir John Nixon in January 1916.

16GW537 Sir John Nixon.

16GW538 Sir Fenton John Aylmer, VC.

General Fenton won the Victoria Cross as a captain in the Royal Engineers in India. His citation reads:

On 2 December 1891, during the assault on Nilt Fort, British India, Captain Aylmer, with the storming party, forced open the inner gate with gun-cotton which he had placed and ignited, and although severely wounded, fired 19 shots with his revolver, killing several of the enemy, and remained fighting until, fainting from loss of blood, he was carried out of action.

16GW539 Sir George Gorringe.

General Nixon gave Lieutenant General Aylmer the task of relieving the siege of Kut. Aylmer's command, the Tigris Corps, consisted of the 7th (Meerut) Division, the 12th (Indian) Division, and various other military units, which amounted to 20,000 men. They left Basra in late December 1915 and arrived at Sheikh Sa'ad 3 January 1916. While the 12th (Indian) Division (under the command of General George Gorringe) made a diversionary move near Nasiriyeh, the 7th (under the command of General Younghusband) staged a direct assault on the Ottoman positions on 6 January (the Battle of Sheikh Sa'ad). After two days of fighting, the Ottoman army withdrew. The British sustained approximately 4,000 casualties. The Ottoman troops, under the command of Baron von der Goltz, withdrew six miles up river and occupied another defensive position near the edge of the Suwaikiya Marshes. A British assault on this position on 13 January 1916 was successful but there were 1,600 casualties.

The 3rd (Lahore) Division was added to Aylmer's command and the Turkish position at Hanna was assaulted. This assault was a failure and 2,700 troops were killed or wounded.

The 13th (Western) Division was further added to Aylmer's command. The next month was spent resting the troops and probing the enemy defensive positions. With time running out for the besieged defenders at Kut, Aylmer finally launched a two pronged attack on 7 March 1916. Both attacks failed. The British suffered 4,000 casualties.

General Aylmer was replaced by the former commander of the 12th Indian division, Lieutenant General Sir George Gorringe. However, by this stage time was running out for the British at Kut.

On 24 April 1916, an attempt by a paddle steamer to resupply the town by river proved unsuccessful. With that failure it became apparent there was to be no relief – the British could not resupply Kut.

After repeated attempts to break out through the ring of besieging Ottomans Townshend surrendered his surviving force of 13,000 men on 29 April 1916.

Many of the British commanders involved in the failed operation to rescue Townshend's division were relieved of command.

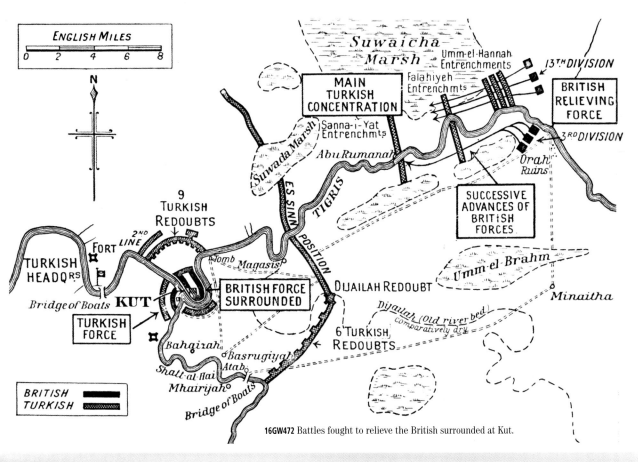

16GW472 Battles fought to relieve the British surrounded at Kut.

16GW542 Indian Cavalry, under the overall command of General Aylmer, advancing to attempt the relief of Kut.
16GW543 Indian army infantry marching alongside the River Tigris towards the Turkish defensive positions blocking the route to Kut.

16GW454 A typical shallow draft boat of the Fly Class, Tigris Flotilla.

16GW544 A Fly Class gunboat on the Tigris providing supporting fire for General Aylmer's relief force fighting towards Kut.

16GW455 A Fly Class gunboat on the Tigris with canvas sun proection from the intense heat.

16GW547 An Australian built motor launch on the Tigris, one of the many and varied craft in use during the campaign in Mesopotamia.

16GW473 On the way up the Tigris, HMS *Espiegle* in action against the Turks, using its 4.7 inch gun.

16GW546 The paddle steamer *Basrah* loaded with Turkish prisoners taken during the fighting to reach the British force trapped at Kut.

16GW545 Transporting Indian troops up the Tigris by paddle boat.

16GW550 As difficult for transport as the mud in Flanders, mules struggle to move this wagon through the desert mud.

16GW549 General Aylmer's relief force, moving north alongside the Tigris, met determined Turkish resistance, incurring heavy casualties. Ambulances, each drawn by a team of six mules, struggle through the sodden desert.

16GW551, 16GW548, 16GW553 Fighting to reach General Townshend's trapped force at Kut, the relief force came up against fierce resistance. British artillery digging in.

A British battery in position before the Battle of Sheik Saad, on the left bank of the Tigris looking towards Kut. General Gorringe launched a determined attack on 7 January, 1916.

16GW552 British artillery officers making the best of a quiet moment before the fighting begins.

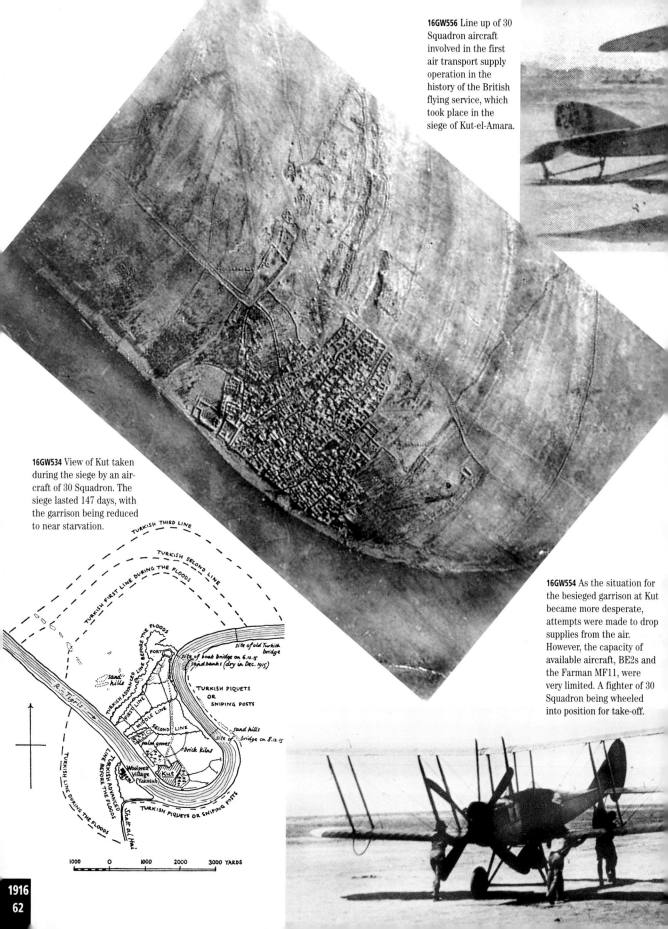

16GW556 Line up of 30 Squadron aircraft involved in the first air transport supply operation in the history of the British flying service, which took place in the siege of Kut-el-Amara.

16GW534 View of Kut taken during the siege by an aircraft of 30 Squadron. The siege lasted 147 days, with the garrison being reduced to near starvation.

16GW554 As the situation for the besieged garrison at Kut became more desperate, attempts were made to drop supplies from the air. However, the capacity of available aircraft, BE2s and the Farman MF11, were very limited. A fighter of 30 Squadron being wheeled into position for take-off.

Aircraft of 30 Squadron, BE2s and Farman MF 11s, dropped 19,000 lbs of food during the months of March and April 1916. This took 140 food-dropping sorties by RFC and Naval aircraft. The load was carried in two 50 lb bags slung each side of the fuselage and a further 25 lb bag was attached to the undercarriage. Because of the prevailing head winds, along with the heavy loads, the cruising speeds of the machines were drastically reduced and they were difficult to control. The aircraft had to be protected by accompanying fighters when German aircraft started intercepting the missions.

16GW577 A Farman MF11.   **16GW475** 'Coolies' carrying an aircraft wing frame into the RFC workshops for repairs.

16GW541 Major General Townshend had no options left – he had to accept defeat and surrender his command to the enemy. The signal was sent at 1.35 pm, 29 April 1916, announcing the end of British resistance at Kut. It was perhaps the most embarrassing episode of the war for British arms.

16GW588 Halil Pasha, 'Hero of Kut'.

Lord Kitchener sent a proposal for the command in Mesopotamia to attempt to buy their troops out of the Kut siege. Aubrey Herbert and T. E. Lawrence were part of a team of officers sent to negotiate a secret deal with the Turks. The British offered to ransom Townshend's troops for one million pounds in silver and a promise that the Division would not be employed in fighting against the Ottomans for the rest of the war. The Turkish commander, Halil Pasha, considered this with some favour, however, Enver Pasha, Minister of War ordered that this offer was to be rejected.

16GW589 Ismail Enver Pasha, Minister of War.

16GW590 T E Lawrence. Two members of the Cairo Intelligence Service, Captain Aubrey Herbert and Captain Thomas Edward Lawrence, were sent to see what could be done to relieve the beleaguered garrison by indirect means. Enver Pasha's rejection of the bribe and promise never to fight against the Turks in future if they were set free meant unconditional surrender for Townshend.

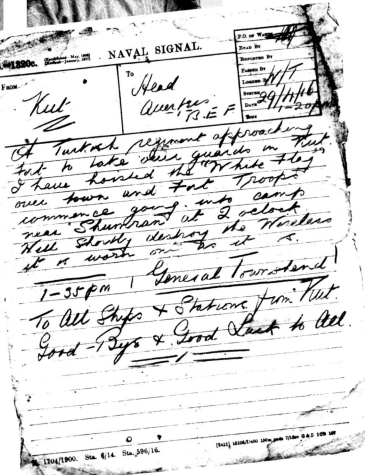

16GW508 Men of the Royal Field Artillery stand by one of their destroyed wagons before the surrender of Kut.

AN EARLY EXAMPLE OF A PROPAGANDA – A MESSAGE CONTAINED IN A TURKISH PAMPHLET CIRCULATED AT KUT DURING THE SIEGE

Oh Dear Indian Brethren.

You understand the fact well that God has created this war for setting India free from the hands of the cruel English. This is the reason why all the Rajahs and Nawabs, with the aid of brave Indian soldiers, are at present creating disturbances in all parts of India and forcing the English out of the country. Consequently not one Englishman is to be seen in the North West Frontier of Indian districts of Saad, Chakdara, Kohmond and Kohet. Brave Indians have killed several of their officers at Singapore, Secunderabad and Meerut contonments. Many of the Indian soldiers have on many occasions joined our allies the Turks, Germans and Austrians, of which you must have heard. Oh heroes our friends the Turks, Germans and Austrians are merely fighting for the freedom of our country from the English and you, being Indian, are fighting against them and causing delay. On seeing your degraded position one feels blood in the eyes that you have not got tired of their disgraceful conduct and hatred for you. You should remember how cruelly Maharajah Ranjit Singh of the Punjab and Sultan Tipu were treated by the British Government, and now, when our beloved country is being released from their cruel clutches, you should no further delay the freedom of your country and try and restore happiness to the souls of your forefathers as you come from the same heroic generation to which the brave soldiers of the Dardanelles and egypt belong. You must have heard about the recent fighting in the Dardanelles when Lord Hamilton was wounded and the cowardly Lord Kitchener ran away at night taking only the British soldiers with him leaving the Indians behind. The Indian soldiers on seeing this murdered all their British officers and joined the Turks. Nearly everywhere we are finding that our Indian soldiers are leaving the British. Is it not a pity that you go on assisting them? Just consider that we have left our homes and that we are fighting for only fifteen or twenty rupees; a subaltern of only twenty or twenty-five years old is drawing a handsome amount as a salary from Indian resources while our old Risaldar [native cavalry commander] and Subadar majors are paid nothing like him – and even a British soldier does not salute them. Is that all the respect and share of wealth we should get for the sake of which we should let them enjoy our country? For instance, see how many of you Indian soldiers were killed during the battle of Ctesiphon and there is nobody to look after the families of the dead and wounded. Brothers, just compare the pay that a British soldier draws with that which you get. Bretheren, hurry up. The British Kingdom is now going to ruin. Bulgaria gave them several defeats; Ireland and the Transvaal have left them but you will already know this. H.M. the Sultan's brave Turkish forces which were engaged on the Bulgar frontier before are now coming over to this side in large numbers for the purpose of setting Indians atliberty. We were forced by the British to leave our beloved country and to live in America, but on hearing the news that our country was being freed from English hands, we came over here via Germany – and found our Indian brethren fighting against our friends the Turks. Brethren, what is done, is done, and now you should murder all your officers and come over and join H.M. Sultan's Army like our brave soldiers did in Egypt. All the officers of this force and Arabs have received orders from H.M. Sultan that any Indian soldier, irrespective of any caste, Sikh, Rajput, Mahratta, Gurkha, Pathan, Shiah or Syed who comes to join the Turks should be granted handsome pay and land for cultivation if he would like to settle in the Sultan's territory. So you must not miss the chance of murdering your officers and joining the Turks to help them restore your freedom.

16GW531 British and Indian rank and file prisoners of war who surrendered at Kut, marching towards Baghdad. They were subjected to cruel treatment and were further deprived when their meagre rations were stolen. At the time of the surrender the strength of the garrison at Kut amounted to 13,309. Some of these were non combatants, so approximately 12,000 British and Indian troops were marched off. Only 30% survived to the end of the war. All but one of the captured officers had been taken up river by boats.

16GW415, 16GW591, Wounded from the fighting at Kut being loaded onto a hospital ship for transporting down river to Amarah or Basra.

16GW456, 16GW457 Hospital Ship No.1, bearing sick and wounded from Kut, coming alongside the bank of the Tigris at Falahiyah.

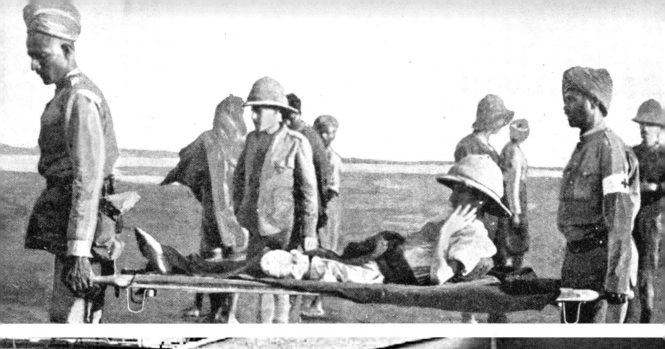

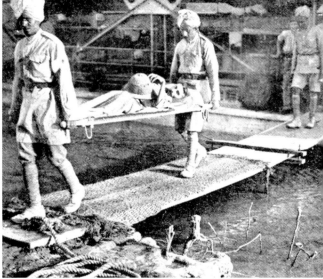

16GW416, 16GW442, 16GW592, 16GW593, 16GW594
Weakened through malnutrition, wounds and disease, these Indian and British troops were released by the Turks after the surrender of Kut. Six boat journeys were made to move the injured down river.

16GW458 A barge loaded with wounded from Kut arriving at Basra.

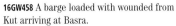

16GW414 Colonel Annesley, ADS & Transport officer on Townshend's staff, arriving at Amarah, among the wounded released by the victorious Turks from Kut.

16GW474 Royal Army Medical Corps boats moored at Amara, with a native boat called a 'Bellum' in use by British soldiers.

16GW485 A British military centre at Amara some distance from Kut-al-Amara.

16GW598 British soldiers enjoying a square meal with a notice saying 'Please keep all refuse off the table'. Covers have to be used to keep flies off the food.

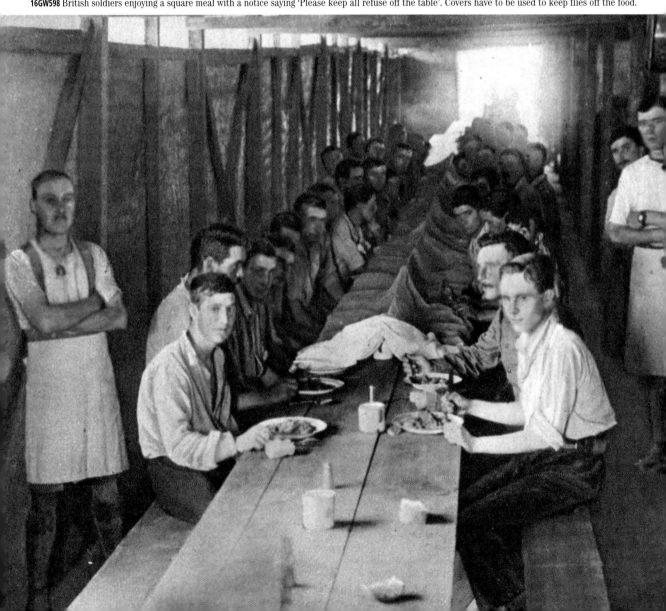

16GW476 A British officer convalescing on the veranda at the military hospital, Amara, after the siege at Kut-al-Amara.

16GW597 British soldiers, less than a week after leaving Kut, putting on weight again at Amara, with pots of tea and bread and jam sandwiches (no one employed to keep the flies off their food, however).

16GW595 These Indian prisoners, suffering from severe malnutrition, have been exchanged for sick Turkish prisoners. Their emaciated condition gave rise to grave concern for all Indian and British prisoners being held in the prisoner of war camps.

16GW484 This cupboard is described as 'an ingenious contrivance designed to keep invalids' food either hot or cold'.

16GW459 Indian soldiers about to board a hospital ship leaving Basra for India.

16GW453 A Graves Registration Officer locating a grave in the old trenches.

16GW507 Turkish commanders pose with their trophies: Major General Townshend and two of his staff, Lieutenant Colonel Parr and Captain Moorland (standing). On Townshend's left is Nizam Bey, who promised that the surrendered officers and other ranks would be treated well. Of the 12,000 British and Indian soldiers taken into captivity some 70% died or were never heard of again. Townshend and his two officers, on the other hand, were treated as honoured guests of the Turks in the capital, Constantinople.

Memorial plaque in the crypt of St Paul's Cathedral

Chapter Two: The Means to Destroy Life

16GW002 The progenitor of all tanks, the Mark I Tank, 'Mother', seen here at Hatfield during early trials 1915 and 1916.

16GW001 A Royal Flying Corps Observer taking on board his 97-round magazines for the defence of his Bristol F2B, introduced in late 1916.

The Birmingham Small Arms company (BSA) and the Daimler Company of Coventry merged in 1910. During the First World War BSA produced rifles, Lewis guns, shells, motorcycles and lorries. During the Boer War a production figure of 2,500 rifles per week was reached. Over a five year period, just prior to the war in 1914, BSA produced 7,000 rifles for the British Government. Shortly after the outbreak of war, output reached 10,000 rifles per week.

16GW003 Rifles and a Lewis light machine gun in a front line trench in Flanders. The men belong to a battalion of the King's Liverpool Regiment.

16GW004 A British sniper, his Short Lee-Enfield fitted with a telescopic sight, keeps watch on the German positions through a trench telescope.

16GW005 Men of a Scottish regiment in action with their Lee-Enfields in some factory ruins.

16GW007 An instructor at the School of Musketry explains the system of charging the rifle magazine using a clip holding five rounds of ammunition.

16GW008 Feeding a clip of five rounds into the magazine of a Lee-Enfield. The magazine held ten rounds.

16GW012 Seaforth Highlanders clearing out a captured German trench at bayonet point.

16GW009 British Service Rifles from 1857 to 1907 manufactured at the Birmingham Small Arms company.

1857
Enfield Rifle – muzzle loader.

1866
1866 Snider Rifle – first British breech loading service rifle; 577 bore.

1870
Martini Rifle – 450 bore.

1888
Lcc Metford – first British magazine rifle; 303 bore.

1907
Lee-Enfield Long – 303 bore with charger bridge guide.

1903
Lee-Enfield Short Mark I, magazine rifle; 303 bore.

1907
Lee-Enfield Short Mark III, magazine rifle; 303 bore.

16GW006 Some war-weary Lee-Enfield rifles salvaged from a battlefield in Flanders.

16GW010 1907 Lee-Enfield Short – Mark III rifle and bayonet.

16GW011 Mauser Gewehr 98 and bayonet. Issued to the German armies of Prussia, Saxony and Württemberg.

16GW013 Stacks of beech and walnut wood, which was dried out for three years for use in the construction of rifle butts and stocks at the BSA factory.

16GW021 The rifle assembly section at Birmingham Small Arms Company.

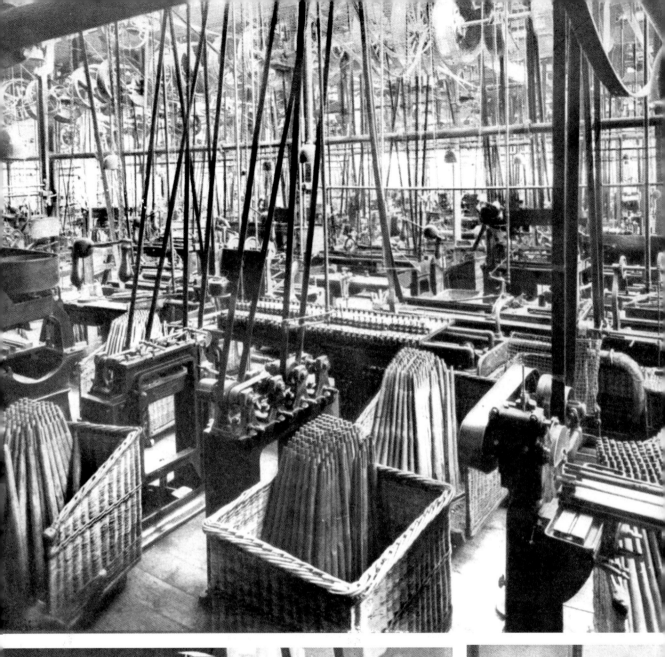

16GW014 Part of the rifle stock making section of B.S.A.

16GW015 Cutting out rifle butts.

16GW016 A lathe for turning rifle butts from the rough cut wood.

16GW020 A barrel truing machine.

16GW022 The first shooting test.

16GW019 The smithy shop, where gun barrels are being forged.

16GW017 Rods for barrels and rifle bolts in storage.

16GW025 An examiner measuring rifle bolts for accuracy.

16GW023 Sighting up a Lee Enfield with the aid of a telescope.

16GW018 The mill for turning barrels.

16GW026 Rifle bores being checked by a Government examiner.

16GW024 A Government inspector testing a rifle's accuracy at a range of 600 yards.

The Lewis gun was invented by US Army Colonel Isaac Newton Lewis in 1911. His design was rejected by the US Government and, after resigning from the army in 1913, he moved to Belgium, where he set up his own production company, Armes Automatique Lewis. The Birmingham Small Arms Company purchased a licence to manufacture the Lewis machine gun in England, which resulted in Colonel Lewis receiving significant royalty payments. The onset of the First World War increased demand for the Lewis gun, and BSA began production under the designation Model 1914. The design was officially approved for service on 15 October 1915 and began being issued to troops in early 1916.

The Lewis gun was much lighter and less cumbersome than both the Maxim and Vickers machine guns, making it easier to move from one position to another quickly. A further advantage of the Lewis was that six of these guns could be made in the time taken to produce one Vickers gun. The Lewis gun was extensively used on British and French aircraft during World War I, as either an observer's or gunner's weapon.

16GW029 Colonel Isaac Newton Lewis,
12 October, 1858 – 9 November, 1931.

16GW028 Lewis gun with carrying handle.

16GW032 RFC observers being issued with machine guns by an officer in the Royal Scots.

16GW027 Lewis guns mounted in the front cockpit of a F.E.2d.

16GW030 Fighter plane with twin Lewis guns for use by the Observer. Note the Vickers machine gun mounted on the wing.

16GW033 Before taxiing for take-off, this crew pose for the camera. The Lewis gun is mounted on a Scarff ring.

16GW031 A Royal Flying Corps armourer issuing Lewis guns to observers.

16GW040 An aircraft pattern Lewis gun, with the distinctive outer barrel case removed.

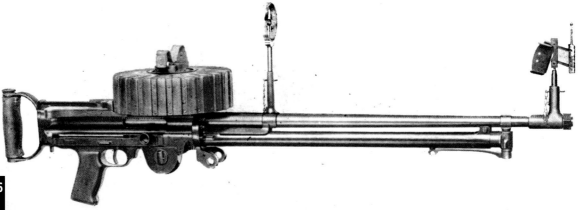

16GW039 An aircraft pattern Lewis gun with the 97-round magazine. The barrel has been fitted with a wind vane to assist in aiming correction.

16GW041 'Aircraft approaching – Friend or Foe?' These Tommies line up their Lewis gun in the anti aircraft role.

16GW034 Forging the radiator case locking piece of the Lewis gun.
16GW035 A worker operating a press for stamping out Lewis gun magazines.
16GW036 The barrel mill where barrels, aluminium radiators and gun bodies were drilled.

16GW037, 16GW037a BSA machine for charging a Lewis gun magazine; also an example of a deep type for aircraft.

16GW038 Test firing Lewis guns on the BSA 100 yards' range.

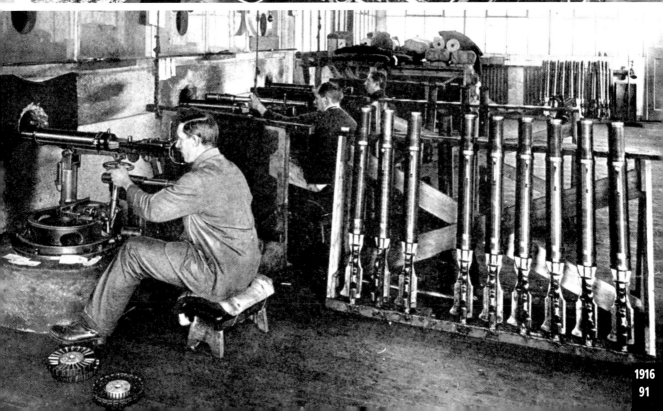

David Lloyd George gained a powerful reputation with his energetic work as Minister of Munitions, 1915–1916. Public opinion had been outraged when the British Army ran short of shells during the fighting in 1915. Demands grew for a strong leader to take charge of munitions. It was agreed that the man for the task was Lloyd George and he was made Minister of Munitions in a new department, created following the near disastrous munitions shortage which had occurred during the two major British offensives in Flanders in 1915. In this position he won much acclaim, which formed the basis for his political progress. He boosted British morale and focused attention on an urgent need for greater output from the new factories that had been established and from the extensions to existing foundries that were being undertaken at all the large arms manufacturers. Reforms, already underway when he took office, were reinforced. The Ministry for Munitions broke through the bureaucracy of the War Office. Lloyd George resolved labour problems, rationalised the supply system and overall war production underwent a dramatic increase. In June 1916 he became Secretary of State for War, succeeding Lord Kitchener, who was killed when his ship, HMS *Hampshire*, on which he was traveling to Russia, struck a mine.

16GW051 A day's castings of rough forgings of 15-inch shells.

16GW043 Rough forgings being rolled to the end of the shop.

16GW044 A shell turning shop with rows of lathes and rough forgings.

16GW045 Turning a shell to bring it to the specified diameter to fit the 15-inch gun barrel.

16GW047 Rough casted shells awaiting turning to smooth the outer casing.

16GW046 Shell being lifted from the lathe after the outside has been rendered smooth in the process of bringing it to the required bore.

16GW049 Fixing copper bands to shells by means of a hydraulic press.

16GW050 Boring out the inside of shells in preparation to take explosives.
16GW054 Dipping shells in tanks containing petrol to clean them.

16GW055 Varnishing the inside of 15-inch shells.

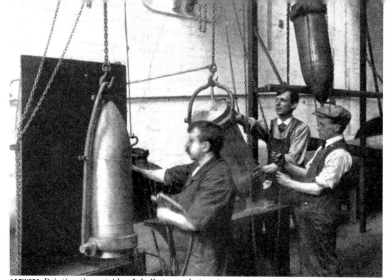

16GW056 Painting the outside of shells to combat rust.

16GW057 Rolling newly painted shells into drying cabinets.

16GW052 Shells leaving Government inspectors.

16GW058 Finished shells in bond ready for despatch.

16GW053 Government inspectors checking the quality of finished 15-inch shells.

16GW042 A railway siding with train and wagons inside the finished shells store.

16GW059 Increasingly women workers were employed to take the place of men joining the forces. These women have been trained to operate lathes as turners.
16GW060 Women at work on small capstan lathes.

16GW066 BSA Cycle Department re-tooled and equipped to produce 18-pounder shells.Railway siding through the finished shells store.

16GW061 Women engaged as inspectors in a small parts machine shop.

16GW062 Female labour in an aircraft engine testing shop.

16GW063 A female operative working an electrical crane in an aircraft engine production shop.

16GW069 B.E.12 aeroplanes being assembled.

16GW070 Twelve cylinder R.A.F 4a aeroplane engines assembly line.

16GW068 Women assembling the wooden frames for aeroplane wings.

16GW072 Assembling nine-cylinder radial engines.

16GW067 Aircraft wing production being carried out by women at the Daimler Company.

16GW071 A single-seater R.E.8 fighter built by the Daimler Company.

16GW079 A tractor hauling a trailer with a crate containing an aeroplane bound for an RFC squadron.

16GW073 The 105 h.p. Daimler tractor.
16GW075 Building engines to drive a new British secret weapon – the tank.

16GW077 Engine and transmission, the power unit for the new weapon.

16GW078 The secret of the tanks was well kept and when they arrived on the battlefield during the Somme offensive they proved to be a considerable shock to the Germans. One of the very first Mk I tanks produced, seen here with Russian lettering, as it was destined for shipment to that country as a trusted and faithful ally.

16GW076 Transmission gear assembly line for tractors and tanks.

16GW080 Eight new tractors ready for delivery to the British Admiralty.

16GW081 Special wagons for conveying gun parts being pulled by a Daimler tractor.

16GW083 Recently completed Daimler lorries ready for delivery to a Government depot.

16GW085 A Daimler truck, kitted out as a mobile workshop, ready to move off.

16GW084 A Daimler mobile workshop in the transport lines of a unit.

16GW082 Troops boarding Daimler lorries for transport to the front. The lack of steel helmets suggests a 1915 photograph.

16GW086 Damaged vehicles brought to the Heavy Repairs Depot.

16GW087 Lorries salvaged after being caught in a German bombardment.

16GW088 Wrecked Daimler lorries following a bombardment.

16GW089 A fleet of new Daimler ambulances having recently arrived at the Medical Corps' Depot.

16GW092 A presentation Daimler ambulance in Paris, presented by the Empress of Russia.

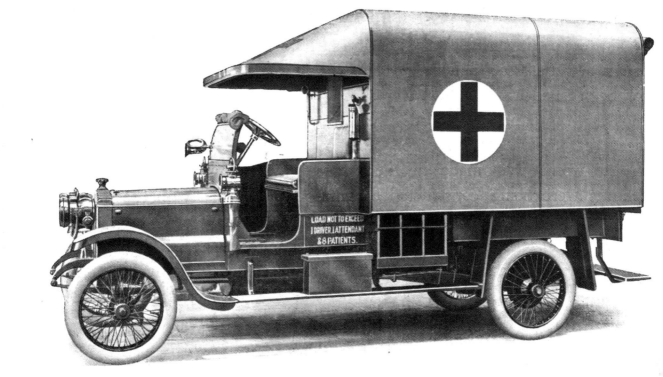

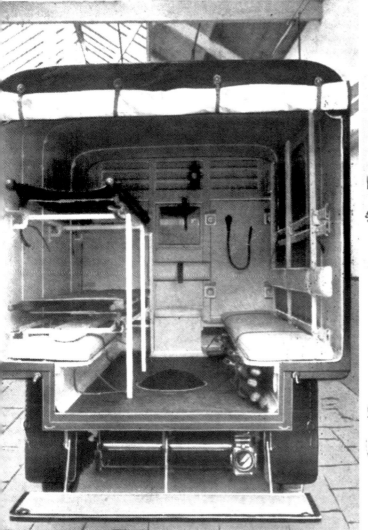

16GW094 The Daimler ambulance coachwork mounted on a 20 h.p. chassis.
16GW095 Interior layout of a Daimler ambulance.
16GW096 King George V's presentation ambulance.
16GW097 Queen Mary's presentation ambulance.

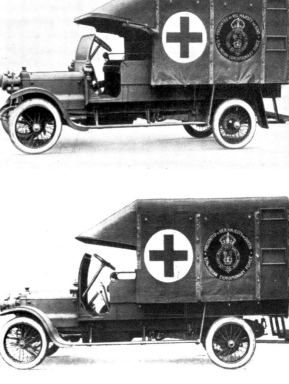

16GW093 Staff cars picking up walking wounded from a hospital ship.
16GW099 A Daimler staff car is stopped at a French checkpoint, 'somewhere in France'.
16GW090 The Daimler staff limousine.

16GW098 A Daimler staff car in service with the Belgian Army.

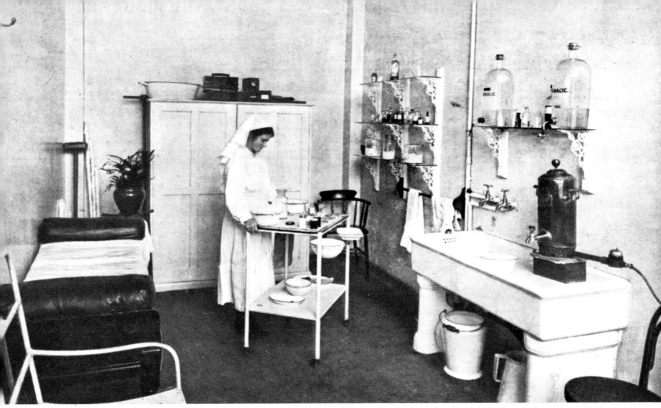

16GW064 A First Aid room at one of the Daimler factories. The enormous increase in the number of employees, unskilled and semi-skilled, necessitated more elaborate means of dealing with accidents. Trifling accidents were inseparable from munition production and records show that forty or fifty cases occurred every day, the majority of which were cuts and bruises. More serious injuries were taken to local hospitals by Company ambulances.

16GW065 The surgery at the Sparkbrook Works.

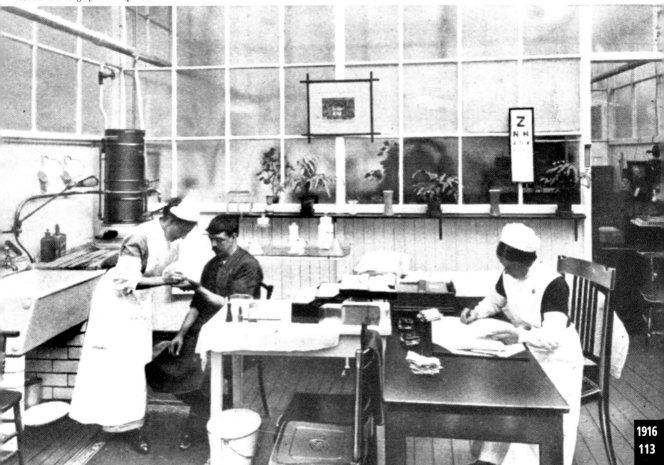

16GW100 A Birmingham Small Arms company Ambulance ready to transport an injured workman to hospital.

Chapter Three: **Verdun – Battles of Attrition**

16GW103 German infantry: one about to throw a stick grenade and another with a Maxim 08/15, belt fed, firing 600 rounds per minute.

16GW102 French machine gun team operating a Hotchkiss gun, which was fed by a 30-round strip and could fire 600 rounds per minute.

The Battle of Verdun was fought from 21 February – 18 December 1916 on hills north of Verdun-sur-Meuse. The German Fifth Army attacked the defences of the Région Fortifiée de Verdun and those of the French Second Army garrisons on the right bank of the Meuse, with the intention of capturing the high ground from which the city of Verdun could be overlooked and bombarded with observed artillery fire. The German strategy was to provoke the defenders into counter offensives to drive them off the heights. The Germans had sufficient artillery massed in the area, along with railway supported supply lines, to defeat French counter attacks. This strategy assumed that the French would attempt to hold on to the east bank of the Meuse, then commit their reserves to recapture it. They would, of course, suffer catastrophic losses from artillery fire, while the German infantry held positions designed to easily ward off all counter attacks. So the reasoning of the German High Command went.

16GW105 French troops under shell fire.

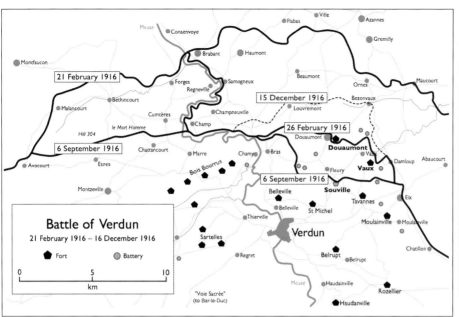

16GW106 Erich Georg Anton von Falkenhayn.

As Chief of the German General Staff, Falkenhayn, entertained the belief that a massive slaughter would lead France's political leaders to consider ending the war. He was convinced that losses would be less harmful for Germany than for France. More than a quarter of a million soldiers were sacrificed to his callous strategy. He was relieved in August 1916.

16GW355 German infantry moving into the Verdun sector, early 1916.

16GW109 Review of troops amassed for the attack on the French defences at Verdun.

16GW107 Kaiser Wilhelm II and the Crown Prince at the Western Front, February 1916.

16GW153 Marching to attack positions for the assault on the French forts.

16GW213 A sapper belonging to a pioneer battalion has a flamer-thrower tube on his back pack. These weapons were first used at Verdun in the German attack on Fort Vaux, June 1916.

16GW108 Crown Prince Wilhelm commanded the German Fifth Army, which was given the task of attacking the French town of Verdun thereby bringing the French army into a battle of attrition. Seen here exchanging a joke with some of his men before the battle.

16GW157 German troops leaving their billets to go to the front.

16GW351 German heavy siege gun being readied for firing on French positions.

16GW157 German troops of a Guards regiment wearing the newly issued steel helmets.

16GW147 Battery of German 180 mm long range guns trained on the French lines.

16GW191 An observation tower built by the Germans to spot for their artillery.

16GW111 A German 21 cm howitzer.

16GW215 A German 15 cm howitzer at Verdun.

16GW387 Mounted on a railway carriage, this German 38 cm gun was used to bombard the forts defending Verdun.

16GW163 Verdun under German artillery fire.

16GW169 A panorama of the almost deserted city of Verdun, with its buildings beginning to show damage from artillery fire.

16GW129 A French memorial to the defenders of Verdun, fighting which took place during the Franco-Prussian War in 1870-1871.

As part of his plan for the unification of Germany, the Chancellor of Prussia, Otto von Bismarck, engineered this war against the France of the Second Empire under Napoleon III. In a matter of weeks the Prussians and their allies had won a series of spectacular victories, leading to Napoleon's abdication and the establishment of the French Third Republic, followed by the Siege of Paris and the abortive revolution of the Paris Commune. In 1871 a unified Germany, dominated by Prussia, was proclaimed, eclipsing France as the major power in Europe. Thus a legacy of rivalry and hatred was sown that was not finally resolved until the end of the Second World War.

In the Second World War the memorial was blown-up by German engineers.

16GW184 The Citadel Errard Bar-le-Duc, Verdun. The citadel was intended to halt the Germans if they broke through on the right bank of the Meuse. During the fighting, the place was mostly used as a shelter for the troops going up to the front and those who returned for rest. It could house up to 6,000 soldiers.

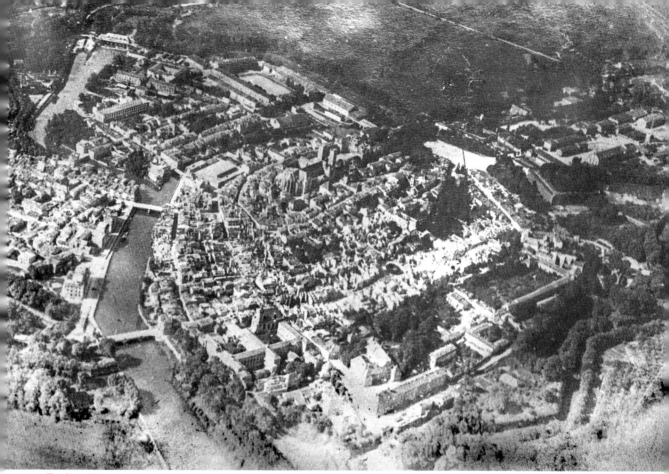

16GW113 The City of Verdun in 1916.

16GW185 The Citadel at Verdun in 1916.

16GW117 The original caption:
A scene on the Meuse, well within the French lines. The Meuse at Verdun is the centre of the great battle.
This section of it is within the French lines and shows a busy riverside scene with women washing clothes whilst a Cavalry Regiment waters the horses.

16GW333 The gate and bridge into the city of Verdun.

16GW187 The Porte and the Pont Chaussée in 1916.

16GW186 Dwellings along the banks of the River Meuse destroyed in the shelling of Verdun in 1915 and 1916.

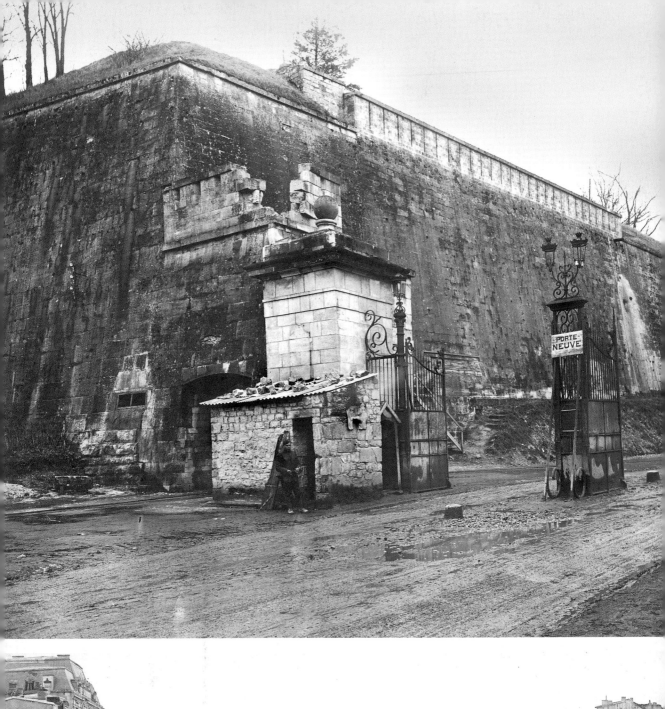

16GW170 Ruins of the Cathedral buildings, Verdun.

16GW140 Cathedral of Notre Dame, Verdun, with ruins extending to the banks of the Meuse.

16GW124 Porte Neuve, Verdun.

16GW125 A bank of the River Meuse, which runs through the city of Verdun.

16GW131 Original caption:
The Huns cannot take Verdun but are still bombarding the town and surroundings with high explosive shells. This photograph shows the most recent condition to which their destructive fury has reduced the Cathedral.

16GW132 Porte Neuve, Verdun.

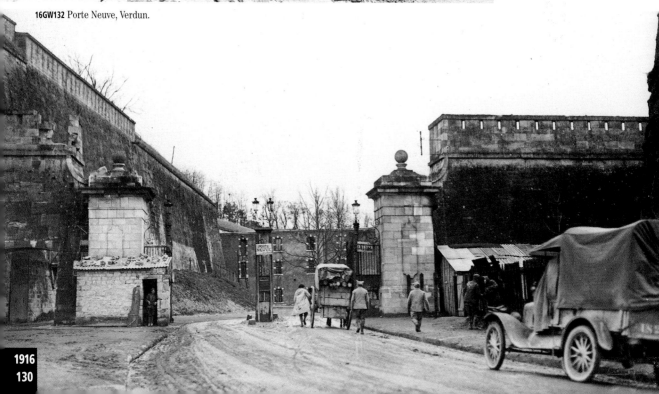

16GW121 The River Meuse running through the battered city of Verdun.

16GW130 Original caption:

The photograph describes the only success the German Crown Prince can take to his credit at Verdun, namely that of smashing the historic city to ruins. The picture shows one of the chapels of the Cathedral.

16GW341 The St Paul Gate, Verdun.

16GW181 French troops marching through the ruins.

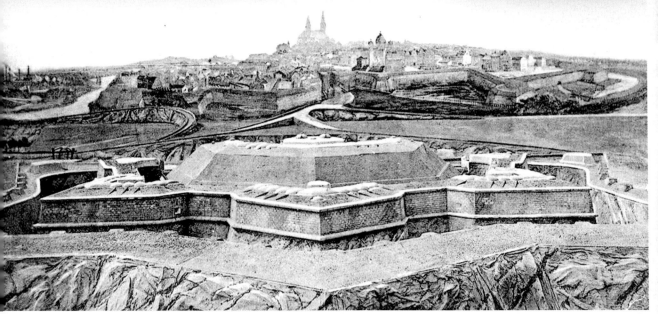

16GW219 Verdun Citadel, with the cathedral (Cathédrale Notre-Dame de Verdun) on the skyline having been, inaccurately, given spires on the twin towers by the German artist.

The German army launched its offensive against Verdun on 21 February 1916. Douaumont was the largest and highest fort of the two concentric rings of forts protecting the city. Its position made it the keystone to the city's defenses. On 24 February, advancing German formations came within striking distance of Fort Douaumont. However, in spite of this imminent danger, it was only manned by a small holding force of fifty-six garrison troops and some artillerymen. Incredibly, no officers were in command; the highest-ranked soldier in the fort was an NCO named Chenot.

Troops of the German 24th Brandenburg Regiment *(6 Infanterie-Division, III Armeekorps)* approached Fort Douaumont from the north, as a reconnaissance or raiding party. The majority of the French defenders were sheltering in the lower levels of the fort to escape the constant shelling from German guns.

16GW188 Aerial view of Fort Douaumont taken in 1915.

16GW165 Entrance blockhouse to Fort Douaumont after shelling in February 1915.

16GW360 German front line position in the Verdun sector in the winter of 1916.

16GW366 German five-man Maxim machine gun team.

16GW110 German infantry passing through their own wire during an attack on the French lines.

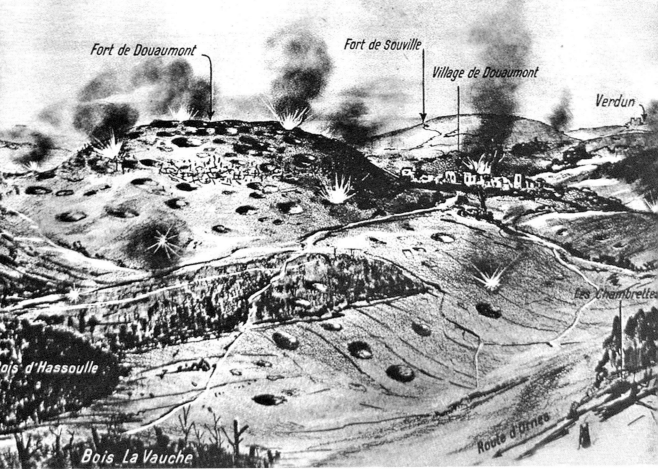

Fort de Douaumont

Fort de Souville

Village de Douaumont

Verdun

Les Chambrettes

Bois d'Hassoulle

Route d'Ornes

Bois La Vauche

16GW348 Artist's drawing of the beginning of the German assault towards the city of Verdun with Fort Douaumont under fire – February 1916.

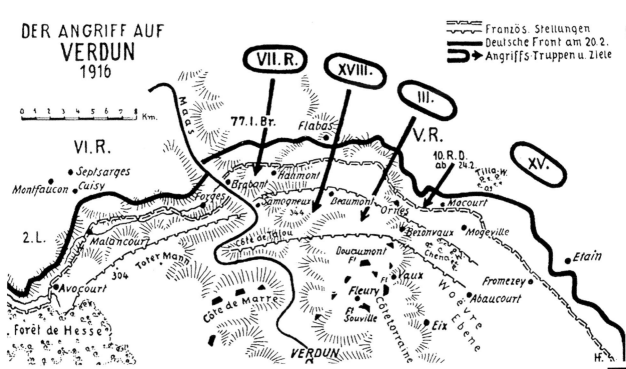

DER ANGRIFF AUF
VERDUN
1916

Franzõs. Stellungen
Deutsche Front am 20.2.
Angriffs·Truppen u. Ziele

VII. R.

XVIII.

III.

V. R.

XV.

0 1 2 3 4 5 6 7 8 Km.

VI. R.

Maas

77.I.Br.   Flabas

Septsarges
Montfaucon Cuisy

Brabant
Forges

Haumont

Samogneux
344

Beaumont Ornes

Côte de Talou

10.R.D.
ab 24.2

Tilla·W.
R.F.P.
ois

Macourt

Mogeville

2. L.

Malancourt

304 Toter Mann

Bezonvaux
Chena

Etain

Douaumont
Ft.

Ft.
Vaux

Woëvre Ebene

Avocourt

Côte de Marre

Fleury

Ft.
Souville

Côte Lorraine

Fromezey

Abaucourt

Eix

Forêt de Hesse

VERDUN

H.

16GW176 German *sturmtruppen* attacking during the Battle of Verdun.

16GW175 German troops using telegraph poles to descend into the ditch at Fort Douamont.

16GW176 German soldiers on top of Fort Douamont af[*] capture.

16GW190 Guard house at Fort Douamont after its capture by the Germans.

16GW313 French soldiers in an underground shelter. Defenders of Fort Douamont were sheltering in the lower levels of the fort when they were captured.

16GW175, 16GW192, 16GW193 Fort Douamont following its capture.

16GW194 Douamont village following its capture in February 1916.

16GW148 German pioneers in an underground shelter.

16GW358 The Germans began the work of shoring up the defences of the captured Fort Douamont.

16GW134 German pioneers in one of their bunkers.

16GW195 An area in the fort used as a hospital and dressing station by the Germans.

16GW179 A kitchen set up in the captured fort.

16GW197 Sleeping quarters; note that these German soldiers have not removed their boots and are thus ready for instant action.

16GW220 German food store in Fort Douaumont, housed in a former water cistern.

16GW200 Seated left, is Hauptmann Frentzen, German engineer officer at Fort Douaumont, from May 1916. He was responsible for defensive improvements.

16GW376 German soldiers taking a break from their labouring on Fort Douaumont's defences.

16GW201 German pioneers clearing a tunnel that has become blocked with debris following the explosion on 8 May, 1916.

16GW221 Fort Douaumont from the air. Before dawn on 8 May 1916, with the Germans in occupation, a gigantic explosion occured deep inside the fort in the southeastern sector. The corridors had been packed with troops at the time awaiting orders to move out and attack the French lines. The death toll was estimated at 700 to 800, with 1,800 injured. The cause of the explosion was never discovered.

16GW180 Casualties from the gigantic explosion that occurred in the depths of Fort Douaumont. The blast tore through the labyrinth of tunnels which were crowded with troops. It had been considered a safe shelter and an infirmary had been sited there. The fort's medical officer described how there were three explosions and the lights went out. This was followed by an terrible roar and an enormous blast which ripped off doors and shook the floor of the infirmary. The explosion had occurred on a lower corridor in the southeastern sector of the fort. It was there that a large number of French 155 mm artillery shells had been stored. A hole about two metres deep had been blown in the floor and the roof had collapsed. The corridors were filled with rubble and mutilated bodies.

16GW222 The northern exit from Artillery Shelter No.1. It was in this shelter that some of the dead killed in the explosion on 8 May, 1916, were buried.

16GW325 German dead gathered for identification and burial.

16GW146, 16GW311 German trenches among the churned up ground.

16GW340 A German newspaper correspondent viewing the terrain at Verdun.

16GW365 A five-man machine gun team pose with their MG 08, which was the standard German automatic weapon in the First World War. It was an adaptation of Hiram Maxim's original 1884 gun.

16GW371 A sap leading to a deep dugout on the Verdun battlefield.

16GW202 Fort Douaumont when occupied by the Germans. This is a photograph of the western ditch.

16GW182 Pioneers of a flamethrower unit. Notice the cuff badge with the skull and cross bones indicating they are *Totenkopfpionire* (skull sappers). They are equipped with Model 1915 flamethrowers. These weapons were employed against the defenders of Fort Vaux in June 1916.

16GW223 German artillery men with gun limbers on the Verdun battlefield.

16GW216 A 25 cm minenwerfer, one of many used to bombard the French positions around Verdun.

16GW345 Fort Vaux from the air, April 1916, with shells exploding on the fort and surrounding trenches.

16GW183 Fort Vaux with French soldiers watching shells explode in the near vicinity.

16GW224 A soldier of an assault battalion wearing a gas mask respirator as protection against gas shells being fired by his own guns.

16GW114 How the fighting around Verdun was explained to the British public in the *Graphic* magazine, May 1916.

16GW122 French prisoners, captured during the fighting at Verdun, being marched off for transporting to Germany.

16GW354 Germans attacking French positions under cover of gas shells.

16GW123 Loading wounded onto a French Red Cross train.

16GW127 Fort Vaux during the fighting with French troops in occupation..

16GW368 A French soldier falls killed or wounded during the fighting at Verdun.

16GW225 French attacking a German trench at Verdun.

16GW326 Every part of the Verdun battleground became covered with unburied dead of both sides as General Falkenhayn's deliberate war of attrition took its course. A German infantryman takes a position next to the partially covered cadaver of a French soldier.

16GW343 The remains of a German *Sturmtrüpper*.

16GW370 General Joffre visiting the French headquarters for the defence of Verdun, situated in the town of Souilly.

16GW379 The town of Souilly, French Army HQ for the Verdun sector.

16GW226 General Joseph Jacques Césaire Joffre. Commander-in-Chief of French forces on the Western Front until the end of 1916.

16GW227 General Philippe Pétain. Commanded the Second Army at the start of the Battle of Verdun in February 1916.

16GW228 General Robert Georges Nivelle. He succeeded Pétain as commander of the French Second Army in the Battle of Verdun,

16GW154 French troops moving up to the support the fighting at Verdun.

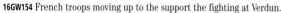

16GW156 French General Guillaumat on the Town Hall steps at Souilly, reviewing troops coming back from the fighting atVerdun.

16GW162 French artillery and infantry heading into the mincing machine of the Verdun battlefield.

16GW230 In May 1916 General Joffre replaced General Pétain with General Nivelle in command of the defence of Verdun.

16GW232 The German Crown Prince with his staff officers. Wilhelm relinquished command of the 5th Army in September 1916.

16GW234 Erich von Falkenhayn. By the summer of 1916 he had been discredited by the bogging-down of the Verdun Offensive and the extent of German losses. In August Hindenburg succeeded him as Chief of the General Staff.

16GW229 General Joffre with General Petain outside the French army headquarters at Souilly.

16GW233 Hindenburg became Chief of the German General Staff in August 1916. He served as the commander-in-chief of the German armed forces rather than the Kaiser. Thus from 1916 Germany effectively became a military dictatorship with Ludendorff and Hindenburg at the head of State.

16GW161 Senegalese soldiers arriving at the Verdun front by train, June 1916.

16GW237 French infantry waiting to be transported to the Verdun front by train.

16GW235 Supplies being transported to the Verdun front.

16GW378 This road, which became known as the 'Sacred Way', was Verdun's main supply route from Bar-le-Duc for the battle.

16GW145 French Infantry dugouts situated alongside the road leading to Verdun.

16GW210 Mules being used to move ammunition to the front.

16GW135 French reserves watching their comrades going into the 'Valley of the Shadow'.

16GW236 French infantry on the march.

16GW152 A French 133 mm gun position with one of the gun crew adjusting a fuse.

16GW150 French quick firing 75 mm field gun housed in the safety of a concrete shelter or 'abri'.

16GW149 French 220 mm trench mortar in action.

16GW155 French 105 mm gun at Verdun.

16GW239, 16GW238 French reserves moving towards Verdun for a counter offensive to drive the Germans back.

16GW120 Original caption: *The Germans thought that in attacking Verdun they were breaking all French efforts and that France, in despair, would have thrown on the Meuse its supreme resources in men, engines and munitions. They were mistaken again. With admirable calm France has proved it. She has fought for five long months in front of Verdun with thousands of men. But France, together with England and Russia, brings into its lines new batteries, new armies and new methods, and in the first weeks of July the initiative of the War has completely passed into the Allies' hands. This gun seen here is undergoing final preparations before it is moved by train for use at the front. We have already seen the results of this artillery which, jointly with the British guns, is bringing victory to the Allies. Our picture shows these guns can be deployed to any part of the front line with relative ease.*

16GW118 Men of a French regiment waiting the order to advance and assault German positions.

16GW243 German 15 cm field howitzer.

16GW242 French trench mortar, having just fired its projectile.

16GW245 A German 15 cm field howitzer which has received a direct hit, destroying a wheel and shrapnel shield.

16GW138 A French 155 mm gun bringing down fire on the German positions.

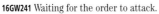

16GW241 Waiting for the order to attack.
16GW337 Leaving the trench.
16GW240 Struggling through their own wire.
16GW324 Entering No Man's Land.

16GW367 Among the ruins of the recaptured Fort Douaumont October 1916.
16GW349 Resting among the ruins of a captured German position.

16GW244 German soldiers surrendering to French infantry.

16GW206 Trenches from where a French attack on German positions set out. Some were caught by German machine-gun fire.

16GW141 German prisoners under French guard. The original caption asserts that they were treated humanely.

16GW119 German prisoners being used to stretcher wounded away to the rear.

16GW209 Near Fort Douaumont after it was recaptured. This fortification, known as Four Chimneys Shelter, was used by the French as an aid post.

16GW373 Fort Douaumont, occupied once more by French troops.

16GW171 Keeping a watcful eye on the German trenches.

16GW208 A gun turret at Fort Souville. It was from here that the French commander, General Mangin directed the successful French attack on Fort Douaumont.

16GW309 French artillery officers observing German troop movements form Côte 304 (Hill 304).

16GW318 The dreadful conditions appear to be making day-to-day living miserable for these soldiers.

16GW322 Manning a trench at Fleury.

16GW303 Typical landscape at Verdun.

16GW144 Typical landscape at Verdun – the remains of a wood.

16GW310 French infantry about to assault a German position.

16GW16GW167, 353 French stretcher bearers resting in this aid post inside a recaptured fort.

16GW319 French infantry in a captured German position.

16GW143 French soldiers sleeping in a trench after winning the ground from the Germans.

16GW246 Walking wounded awaiting darkness to leave for the rear and hospital treatment.

16GW207 French infantry seen here during an attack to dislodge the enemy.

16GW112 French infantry seeking to remove the Germans from their well built positions on the dominating hill known as le Mort Homme (so named from a time prior to the Great war).

The bombardment hurled at the forts and French lines had so thoroughly smashed up the ground that any continuing German advance to the city of Verdun became nigh on impossible. Throughout their offensive the range of hills to the northwest of Verdun, on the left bank of the Meuse, provided positions from which French artillery could pound the flanks of the German infantry advancing on the other side of of the river. The order was given on 6 March, by the commander, Crown Prince Wilhelm, for the infantry to attack the ridge of hills to stop this enfilading fire. Gains were made at first, but the attack on Mort Homme was held by determined French resistance. The French fought back aided by artillery and machine-gun fire from their positions on Hill 304 (Cote 304). However, by the end of May both Hill 304 and Mort Homme fell to the attackers. They also took the small village of Cumières, but this was as far as the Germans were to reach on the left bank in the Battle of Verdun.

16GW248 Germans in a well constructed defensive position on the high ground in the le Mort Homme sector.

16GW249 Pack animals carrying ammunition up to the German infantrymen in the autumn of 1916.

16GW330, 16GW327 The Kronprinz Tunnel under Mort Homme after its capture by the French.

16GW250 Storm troops negotiating their way along a muddy overflow trench on their way to the front.

16GW372 French soldiers consolidating one of the recaptured forts.

16GW338 The hilly landscape around Verdun.

16GW126 Entrance to a German dugout in one of the recaptured forts.

16GW334 The bodies of French soldiers flung about like rag dolls after a fierce and accurate bombardment.

16GW133 Fort Vaux after the fort's recapture by the French after the Germans withdrew on 2 November 1916.

16GW139 Fort Vaux: after months of fierce fighting and bombardment, it had pounded the concrete until it resembled natural rock.

16GW115 The original caption read: *This photograph was taken immediately after the first French troops had reoccupied Fort Vaux and shows two French soldiers undertaking the most dangerous task in this war – carrying despatches across No Man's Land into the fort to which there was only one entrance. The others had all been smashed by shells.*

16GW301 Work on fortifying the ruins of Fort Vaux carried on through the night following its occupation by the French in November 1916. Floodlights are in evidence in this photograph.

16GW336 A commodity in constant demand by both sides – drinking water. Here French troops are collecting water from large storage barrels.

16GW156 French soldiers awaiting the next attack.

16GW308 French infantry of 363e Regiment pause for the camera before marching on to positions around the city of Verdun. This makes for an interesting study of their uniforms and equipment. The bayonet was called 'Rosalie' by the men.

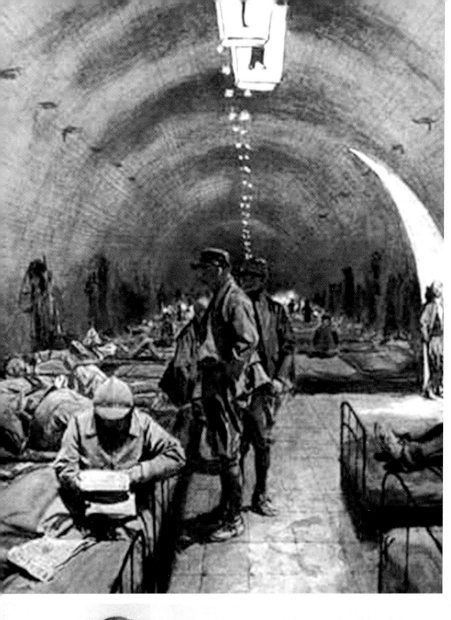

16GW316 A dressing station set up in a retaken fort at Verdun.

16GW377 Outside a dressing station at Verdun.

16GW314 Inside the Citadel at Verdun, where the barracks were in constant use during the fighting.

16GW332 A machine gun set up among the ruins of one of the forts.

16GW375 The concrete mass of Fort Vaux has been transformed by the guns of both sides so as to appear as natural rock. Entrances have lost their gates and been replaced by sandbags.

16GW391 French troops resting on the way to the Verdun battlefields.

16GW392 A soup carrying detail making its way through the trench system.

16GW393 Enjoying the basic food supplied to the Poilu.

16GW331 French soldiers in the ruins of one of the villages. A number of settlements around Verdun were pounded into dust and were never rebuilt, the so called 'villages détruits'.

16GW323 A German machine gun captured in working order at one of the forts. Most likely it would be from Fort Douaumont, as the Germans withdrew in good order from Fort Vaux and thoroughly demolished facilities and gun positions.

16GW261 A French artillery observer watching the fall of shells.

16GW259 A camouflaged 155 mm gun receiving some careful attention from its crew of French gunners.

16GW252 Realigning a 155 mm artillery piece.

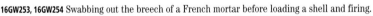

16GW253, 16GW254 Swabbing out the breech of a French mortar before loading a shell and firing.

16GW205 Bombarding German positions at Verdun; this 370 mm French railway gun has just fired a shell.

16GW251 The original caption: *His bark is awful, but his bite is worse ...Verdun has been a mighty triumph for France's artillery.*

16GW262 The original caption: *Monster vials of wrath to be despatched across to the German lines as soon as they arrive.*

16GW260 French gunners loading a quick-firing artillery piece.

16GW255 Some of the thousands of French troops flooding into the Verdun area to reinforce the massive defensive battle being fought out.

16GW258 A French newsvendor selling his wares in the battle area.

16GW256 A peaceful scene in the environs of Verdun. Poilus resting after a spell in the trenches. We are told: ... *not in the least discouraged by their exposure to the devilries of liquid fire and poison gas.*

16GW263 The caption reads: *French soldiers prepare a warm welcom for the Boches.*

16GW257 The caption informs us: *Part of the day's catch of German prisoners taken in the Verdun area.* Trains are taking them to camps in western France.

16GW266 A genuine action picture published in the *New York Tribune*, showing French infantry passing through their own barbed wire to attack the German positions. Note the leather ammunition pouches and canvas bomb satchels. Compare with the posed picture opposite.

16GW265 An action picture posed for the cameraman. Note the full marching kit being worn, including the spare pairs of boots, mess tins and blankets. Not encumberment normally worn when engaging the enemy.

16GW282 Fresh troops on the way into the 'mincing machine' of Verdun arrive at the safe limit of the motor transport. Go further and German artillery spotters would signal the guns.

16GW283 More scowls than smiles from these Poilus resting and awaiting their breakfasts to be prepared.

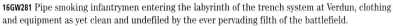
16GW281 Pipe smoking infantrymen entering the labyrinth of the trench system at Verdun, clothing and equipment as yet clean and undefiled by the ever pervading filth of the battlefield.

16GW268 A Poilu writes a letter home.

16GW264 Original caption: *A pair of French soldiers keeping guard over a passage torn through this natural barricade.*

16GW295 Attempting to draw enemy fire, these soldiers hope to entice a German marksman to fire at their dummy. Spotters, either side along the trench, will try to locate the sniper's position.

16GW294 These French reservists manifest a disinclination to acknowledge the cameraman, perhaps viewing him as an intruder.

16GW267 Rarely ever a smile for the camera – these French soldiers carry on with their meal.

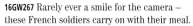

16GW274 An all-out attack by the Germans is imminent – there has been a gas alert.

16GW279 German *Sturmtruppen* killed in the French trenches.

16GW273 Germans appearing through the gas and smoke.

16GW276 German reserves wearing protection against their own poisonous fumes being released to drift in waves towards the French positions.

16GW284 Some meagre protection for this Poilu.

16GW272 French troops attacking across No Man's Land.

16GW285 Gathering the wounded and consolidating the captured German trenches.

16GW286 French troops resting after a successful assault and capture of German positions at Verdun

16GW277 French wounded await evacuation.

16GW296 A French war dog, Rolf, masked against gas.

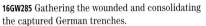

16GW287 Three French fighter aces are posed in the cockpit of a Voisin V. This was a single engined 'pusher' aircraft design with no rearward firing machine gun to defend against a stern attack. The photograph appeared on the cover page of the French magazine *La Guerre Aérienne Illustrée*, 16 November 1916.

The original caption translated reads:

These three champions of hunting, used to dashing machines, manoeuverable and fast, seem a little disoriented in this imposing aircraft armed with a single cannon, powerful and majestic. They are, from left to right, lieutenants Guynemer, Heurteaux and Deullin, the squadron leader. On the 5 November their combined score of downed enemy aircraft numbered 36: Guynemer – our record holder – 18; Heurteaux, 11; Deullin, 7.

Georges Guynemer

Alfred Heurtaux.

Albert Louis Deullin

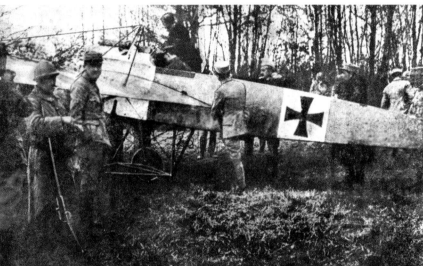

16GW269 A makeshift anti-aircraft weapon has just been completed, having been constructed from a wagon wheel mounted with a strip-fed *mitrailleuse* (machine gun).

16GW271 This German Albatross was brought down at Verdun and landed in one piece. General Joffre examines the machine.

16GW270 The original caption for this German fighter being carefully examined reads: *These sentinels of the air did considerable execution among our more daring aviators until their measure was taken.*

16GW291 A French Nieuport XII shot down by German ace Kurt Wintgens on 20 May 1916. With all the mass slaughter going on there was still sufficient interest to record individual duals being fought by fighter pilots in the air over the blood soaked battlefields.

16GW293 A captured German trench with the bodies of three of the defenders who lost their lives in its defence.

16GW273 The corpses of French soldiers gathered for identification and burial.

16GW278 The body of a French soldier killed at the entrance to his dugout.

16GW280 A remote part of the Verdun battle-field, abandoned by the protagonists and now cluttered with smashed weapons, equipment and human remains. A silent testamony to the callous stupidity of a deliberately sought after and planned battle of attrition.

16GW386 An unusual photograph taken of the victims of a shell explosion with a French soldier posing alongside his dead comrades.

16GW384 A group of attacking infantrymen cut down at the wire.

16GW381 French corpses gathered for identification and burial.
16GW385 A dead French soldier lies where he has fallen.

16GW383 The corpse of a French soldier becoming one with the tortured ground.

16GW390 A dead German Stormtrooper lies among his scattered equipment. The paperwork around him indicates a search to try and find any information that could assist French intelligence.

16GW304 The remains of German soldiers in a trench that has received an accurate rain of shells.

16GW382 A disinternment caused by shelling of the contents of a German trench cemetery.

16GW394 Artist's impression of the fighting at Verdun. Original caption: *A maelstrom of the Meuse; French infantry debouching to attack a flaming ridge near Douaumont.*

16GW398 Erecting a cross over a comrade's grave.

16GW398 German prisoners captured in the Verdun fighting being interrogated by French Staff officers.

16GW395 Material at a depot in the Meuse sector. A network of light railways and firm roads brought in material for the defence of Verdun.

16GW396 Dugouts on the hillside before Verdun.

16GW397 Headquarters of a French division established in a cellar at Verdun.

16GW297 French soldiers being awarded medals in the vicinity of Verdun. Original caption: *Honour for Petain's braves.*

16GW389 German reinforcements, marching to support the fighting at Verdun, acknowledge one of their senior officers. The original caption informs the reader that these are wounded German infantry about to be transported back to their base hospital; however, there is not a bandage in sight.

16GW298 In a French village near Verdun. The original caption reads: *More men to hold the foe at bay; men move forward at the critical hour.*

16GW299 The Crown Prince at the Verdun front. He was nominally in charge of the colossal operations. Note what might well be a lucky horseshoe.

16GW204 A flare illuminates the devasted landscape at Verdun and a soldier freezes, thus becoming a part of the background. Any movement could draw fire.

16GW116 The original caption reads: *The words 'Honour and Countr'' engraved on the French Colours embraces all the Allies are fighting for. Here the tattered flags of a French Division are being paraded in honour of French soldiers who have fought heroically at Verdun. General Gourand, who has lost an arm in the war, is standing in the picture which was taken during his review of the gallant divisions.*

16GW173 Fort Vaux after its reoccupation by the French.

16GW306 French officers of various arms attending prayers of thanksgiving following the recapture of one of the forts.

16GW292 French soldiers happy to be leaving the Verdun area – December 1916.

Information used in this chapter was based on the following titles in the **Battleground Europe** series of guide books:
Fort Douaumont; Fort Vaux; Walking Verdun and *Verdun - The Left Bank* by Christina Holstein
These are available from Pen & Sword History Books Ltd.

Chapter Four: **Jutland – When Battle Fleets Collided**

16GW801 The German High Seas Fleet steaming to action.

16GW802 The Royal Navy's Grand Fleet in the North Sea.

At the outbreak of the Great War a group was formed at the Admiralty, London, that was referred to, mysteriously, as 'Room 40'. The basis of Room 40 operations developed around a German naval codebook, the *Signalbuch der Kaiserlichen Marine* (SKM), and around captured maps. The Russians had seized this material from the German cruiser *Magdeburg* when it ran aground off the Estonian coast on 26 August 1914.

Admiral Scheer had taken command of the German High Seas Fleet in January 1916 and proceeded to take aggressive action against the Royal Navy. With a fleet of 16 dreadnoughts, 6 pre-dreadnoughts, 6 light cruisers, and 31 torpedo boats the German fleet sailed on the morning of 31 May. It was accompanied by a command under Admiral Hipper which comprised 5 battlecruisers and supporting ships.

Room 40 intercepted and decrypted German radio traffic containing plans of the operation. The Admiralty ordered the Grand Fleet, totaling some 28 dreadnoughts and 9 battlecruisers, to intercept and destroy the High Seas Fleet. The scene was set for the clash of naval giants.

16GW803 Vice Admiral Franz Ritter von Hipper, Commander of the fleet reconnaissance forces.

16GW804 Vice Admiral Reinhard Scheer, Commander in Chief of the High Seas Fleet.

16GW805 I and II Squadrons of the *Hochseeflotte* (High Seas Fleet) at their anchorage in Kiel.

16GW806 The High Seas Fleet sailing out to do battle.

16GW807 SMS *König*, the first of four König-class dreadnought battleships. It was the leading ship (and flagship) of the German line on 31 May 1916 at the Battle of Jutland. Commanded by *Kapitän* Brüninghaus.

The four battleships, *König, Grosser Kurfurst, Markgraf* and *Kronprinz* comprised the 5th Division of the *III.Geschwader* (3rd Battle Squadron).

16GW808 SMS *Grosser Kurfurst. Kapitän* Ernst Goette.

16GW809 SMS *Markgraf. Kapitän* Karl Seiferling.

16GW810 SMS *Kronprinz. Kapitän* Constanz Feldt.

16GW811 SMS *Kaiser* (flagship). *Kapitän* Walter von Keyserlingk.

The three battleships, *Kaiser, Prinzregent Luitpold*, and *Kaiserin* comprised the 6th Division of the *III.Geschwader* (3rd Battle Squadron).

16GW812 SMS *Prinzregent Luitpold. Kapitän* Karl Heuser.

16GW813 SMS *Kaiserin. Kapitän* Karl Sievers.

16GW819 Vice Admiral Reinhard Scheer, Commander in Chief of the High Seas Fleet.
16GW814 SMS *Friedrich der Grosse, Flaggschiff der Hochseeflott.* (Fleet Flag Ship). *Kapitän* Theodor Fuchs.

16GW815 SMS *Ostfriesland. Kapitän* Ernst-Oldwig von Natzmer.

The four battleships, *Ostfriesland, Thuringen, Heligoland* and *Oldenburg* comprised the 1st Division of the *I.Geschwader* (1st Battle Squadron).

16GW816 SMS *Thuringen. Kapitän* Hans Küsel.
16GW817 SMS *Heligoland. Kapitän* Frederich von Kameke.
16GW818 SMS *Oldenburg. Kapitän* Wilhelm Höpfner.

16GW820 SMS *Posen* (flagship). *Kapitän* Richard Lange.

The four battleships, *Posen, Nassau, Westfalen* and *Rheinland* comprised the 2nd Division of the *I.Geschwader* (1st Battle Squadron).

16GW821 SMS *Nassau. Kapitän* Robert Künhe.

16GW822 SMS *Westfalen Kapitän* Johannes Redlich.

16GW823 SMS *Rheinlan Kapitän* Heinrich Rohardt.

16GW824 SMS *Deutschland* (flagship). *Kapitän* Hugo Meurer.

The three pre Dreadnought battleships, *Deutschland, Pommern* and *Hessen,* comprised the 3rd Division of the *II.Geschwader* (2nd Battle Squadron).

16GW825 SMS *Pommern. Kapitän* Siegfried Bölken.

16GW826 SMS *Hessen. Kapitän* Rudolf Bartels.

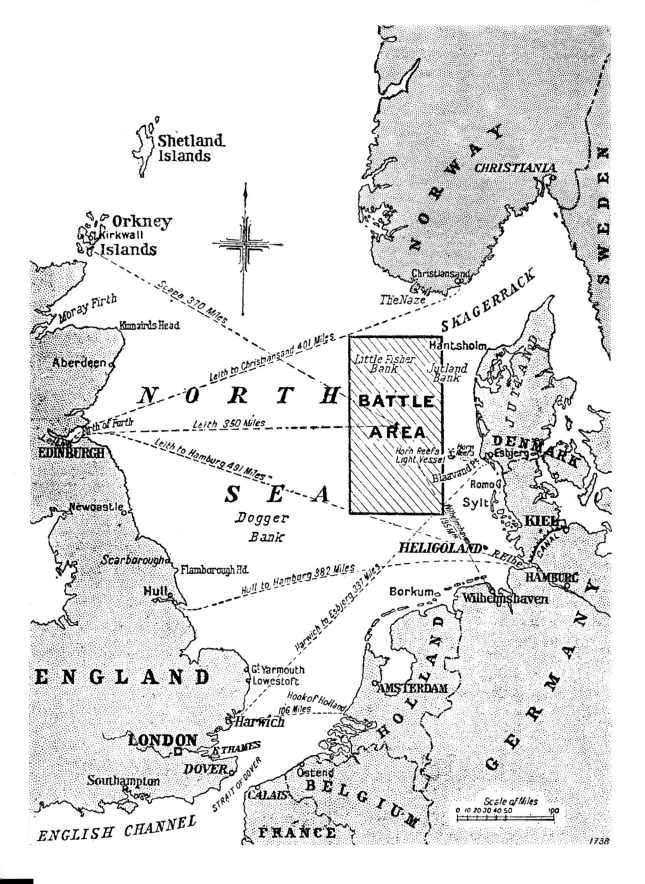

16GW827 SMS *Hannover* (flagship). *Kapitän* Wilhelm Heine.

The three pre Dreadnought battleships, *Hannover, Schlesien* and *Schleswig-Holstein* comprised the 4th Division of the *II.Geschwader* (2nd Battle Squadron).

16GW828 SMS *Schlesien*. *Kapitän* Friedrich Behncke.

16GW829 SMS *Schleswig-Holstein*. *Kapitän* Eduard Varrentrapp.

16GW830 SMS *Stettin* (flagship). *Kapitän* Friedrich Rebensburg.

18GW831 Ludwig von Reuter, commander, 4th Scouting Group

16GW832 SMS *Hamburg*. *Kapitän* Gerhard von Gaudecker.

16GW833 SMS *München.*
Kapitän Oscar Böcker.

The five *Aufklärungsgruppe* (light
cruisers), *Stettin, München,*
Stuttgart, Hamburg and *Frauenlob,*
comprised the 4th Scouting Group.

16GW834 SMS *Stuttgart. Kapitän* Max
Hagedorn.

16GW835 SMS *Frauenlob. Kapitän*
Georg Hoffman.

16GW840 SMS *Seydlitz. Kapitän* Moritz von Edigy.

16GW841 SMS *Derfflinger. Kapitän* Johannes Hartog.

16GW842 SMS *Moltka. Kapitän* Johannes von Karpf.

16GW843 SMS *Von der Tann. Kapitän* Hans Zenker.

16GW844 SMS *Lutzow* (flagship). *Kapitän* Victor Harder.

16GW845 Admiral Hipper (centre) with his staff in 1916. Hipper commanded *I.Aufklärungsgruppe* (1st Scouting Group), which consisted of the battle cruisers:
Lutzow, *Derfflinger*, *Seydlitz*, *Moltka* and *Von der Tann*.
Second from left is Erich Raeder, the future *Großadmiral* during the Second World War.

16GW846 SMS *Frankfurt* (flagship). *Kapitän* Thilo von Trotha.

The four *Aufklärungsgruppe* (light cruisers), *Frankfurt*, *Elbing*, *Pillau* and *Wiesbaden*, comprised the 2nd Scouting Group.

16GW847 SMS *Elbing.* Commander Rudolf Madlung.

16GW848 SMS *Pillau*. Commander Konrad Mommsen.

16GW849 SMS *Wiesbaden*. Commander Fritz Reiss.

Scouting Force Torpedo Boats.

16GW850 SMS *Regensburg*
(light cruiser; flagship,
Leader of Torpedo Boats).
Kapitän Bruno Heuberer.

16GW851 Torpedo boat *S63*.

16GW855 The German High Seas Fleet sailing north to do battle with ship of the Royal Navy.

16GW856 A British radio operator monitoring wireless telegraphy messages using a radio wave Marconi device.

16GW857 Part of the Grand Fleet under Admiral Jellicoe at anchorage at Scapa Flow.

16GW858 Admiral Beatty's squadron anchored at the Royal Naval base in the Firth of Fourth, being overflown by a powered balloon of the Royal Navy.

16GW907 Admiral of the Fleet John Jellicoe.

16GW909 Vice-Admiral David Richard Beatty.

16GW859 A Royal Navy battleship crew line up at the command: 'Splice the main brace'. This was a double ration of rum. A captain could order this after a successful engagement.

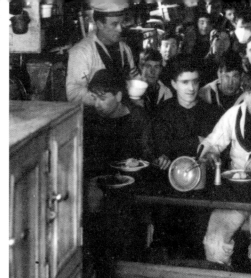

16GW883 British sailors in the cramped quarters of a battleship mess. Few ships had heating closeness would have to do.

16GW880 British sailors enjoying a meal in the cramped quarters of a battleship's mess.

16GW882 Officers playing table bowls in their mess. The ship's mascot looks on, no doubt wondering when he can 'fetch'.

16GW881 Communications room on a British battleship.

The Somme

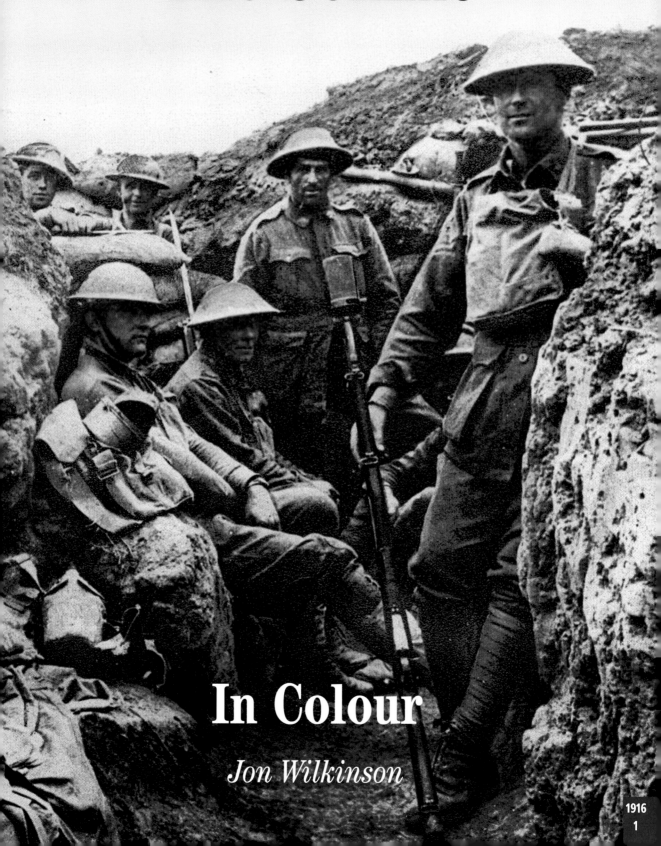

In Colour

Jon Wilkinson

16co02 Men of the Worcestershire Regiment on the Acheux road leading to the trenches, June 1916.

PALS BATTALIONS on THE SOMME

These battalions were made up of men who had enlisted together in local recruiting drives, with the promise that they would be able to serve alongside their friends and work colleagues – their pals (or chums) – rather than being allocated to the many battalions within the regimental system of the Army.

By the end of September 1914, more than fifty towns had formed 'Pals' battalions. The organizers of locally raised units were expected to meet the initial accommodation, feeding and clothing and other costs involved, until the War Office took over their management. The big drawback to the Pals system became obvious with the appaling casualties suffered on the opening day of the Somme battle. The practice of drawing recruits from a particular region or group ensured that, when a Pals battalion suffered heavy casualties, the impact on individual communities in Britain was devastating.

When conscription was introduced in March 1916, the Pals battalions system was no longer considered. Recruitment through civilian authorities outside the regular army structure would never be repeated. The Pals and Chums phenomenon, born of the patriotic jingoism of 1914-15, was unique.

Eight Fourth Army divisions, the **30th**, **31st**, **32nd**, **34th**, **35th**, **36th**, **38th** and **39th**, were made up mainly of Pals battalions for the Big Push. The 38th and 39th were in reserve on the first day. Sprinkled among the Pals divisions were some Regular Army and Territorial Force battalions. This was to stiffen the 'civilian soldiers' in their first big encounter with the Germans.

30th Infantry  Division

89 BRIGADE

2nd Battalion
Bedfordshire Regt
(Regular Army)

17th Battalion
**The King's
(Liverpool Regt)**
(First Liverpool Pals)

19th Battalion
**The King's
(Liverpool Regt)**
(Third Liverpool Pals)

20th Battalion
**The King's
(Liverpool Regt)**
(Fourth Liverpool Pals)

21 BRIGADE

2nd Battalion
**Alexandra Princess
of Wales Own
(Yorkshire Regt)**
Green Howards
(Regular Army)

2nd Battalion
**Duke of Edinburgh's
Own Wiltshire Regt**
(Regular Army)

18th Battalion
**The King's
(Liverpool Regt)**
(Second Liverpool Pals)

19th Battalion
Manchester Regt
(Fourth Manchester Pals)

90 BRIGADE

2nd Battalion
Royal Scots Fusiliers
(Regular Army)

16th Battalion
Manchester Regt
(First Manchester Pals)

17th Battalion
Manchester Regt
*(Second Manchester
Pals)*

18th Battalion
Manchester Regt
(Third Manchester Pals)

11th Battalion (Pioneers)
**Prince of Wales's Volunteers
(South Lancashire Regt)**
(St Helen's Pioneers)

31st Infantry Division

92 BRIGADE

10th Battalion
East Yorkshire Regt
(Hull Commercials)

11th Battalion
East Yorkshire Regt
(Hull Tradesmen)

12th Battalion
East Yorkshire Regt
(Hull Sportsmen)

13th Battalion
East Yorkshire Regt
(Hull T'others)

93 BRIGADE

15th Battalion
West Yorkshire Regt
(Leeds Pals)

16th Battalion
West Yorkshire Regt
(First Bradford Pals)

18th Battalion
West Yorkshire Regt
(First Bradford Pals)

18th Battalion
Durham Light Infantry
(Durham Pals)

94 BRIGADE

12th Battalion
York & Lancaster Regt
(Sheffield City)

13th Battalion
York & Lancaster Regt
(First Barnsley Pals)

14th Battalion
York & Lancaster Regt
(Second Barnsley Pals)

11th Battalion
East Lancashire Regt
(Accrington Pals)

12th Battalion (Pioneers)
**King's Own Yorkshire Light
Infantry**
(Wakefield & Pontefract Miners)

32nd Infantry Division

14 BRIGADE

1st Battalion
Dorsetshire Regt
(Regular Army)

2nd Battalion
The Manchester Regt
(Regular Army)

15th Battalion
Highland Light Infantry
(Glasgow Tramways)

19th Battalion
Lancashire Fusiliers
(Third Salford Pals)

96 BRIGADE

2nd Battalion
Royal Inniskilling Fusiliers
(Regular Army)

15th Battalion
Lancashire Fusiliers
(First Salford Pals)

16th Battalion
Lancashire Fusiliers
(Second Salford Pals)

16th Battalion
Northumberland Fusiliers
(Newcastle Pals)

97 BRIGADE

2nd Battalion
King's Own Yorkshire Light Infantry
(Regular Army)

11th Battalion
Border Regt
(Lonsdale Pals)

16th Battalion
Highland Light Infantry
(Glasgow Boys' Brigade)

17th Battalion
Highland Light Infantry
(Glasgow Chamber of Commerce)

17th Battalion (Pioneers)
Northumberland Fusiliers
(North Eastern Railway)

34th Infantry Division

101 BRIGADE

10th Battalion
Lincolnshire Regt
(Grimsby Chums)
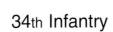

11th Battalion
Suffolk Regt
(Cambridgeshire)

15th Battalion
Royal Scots (Lothian Regt)
(First Edinburgh)

16th Battalion
Royal Scots (Lothian Regt)
(Second Edinburgh)

102 BRIGADE

20th Battalion
Northumberland Fusiliers
(First Tyneside Scottish)

21st Battalion
Northumberland Fusiliers
(Second Tyneside Scottish)

22nd Battalion
Northumberland Fusiliers
(Third Tyneside Scottish)

23rd Battalion
Northumberland Fusiliers
(Fourth Tyneside Scottish)

103 BRIGADE

24th Battalion
Northumberland Fusiliers
(First Tyneside Irish)

25th Battalion
Northumberland Fusiliers
(Second Tyneside Irish)

26th Battalion
Northumberland Fusiliers
(Third Tyneside Irish)

27th Battalion
Northumberland Fusiliers
(Fourth Tyneside Irish)

18th Battalion (Pioneers)
Northumberland Fusiliers
(First Tyneside Pioneers)

35th [Bantam] Division

104 BRIGADE

17th Battalion
Lancashire Fusiliers
*(First South
East Lancashire)
(Bantam Battalion)*

18th Battalion
Lancashire Fusiliers
*(Second South
East Lancashire)
(Bantam Battalion)*

20th Battalion
Lancashire Fusiliers
*(Fourth Salford Pals)
(Bantam Battalion)*

23rd Battalion
Manchester Regt
*(Eighth City)
(Bantam Battalion)*

105 BRIGADE

14th Battalion
**Glouchestershire
Regiment**
*(West of England)
(Bantam Battalion)*

15th Battalion
**Sherwood Foresters
(Nottinghamshire &
Derbyshire Regt)**
(Nottingham) (Bantam Battalion)

15th Battalion
Cheshire Regt
*(First Birkenhead)
(Bantam Battalion)*

16th Battalion
Cheshire Regt
*(Second Birkenhead)
(Bantam Battalion)*

106 BRIGADE

17th Battalion
**Royal Scots
(Lothian Regt)**
*(Rosebury)
(Bantam Battalion)*

17th Battalion
**Prince of Wales's Own
(West Yorkshire Regt)**
*(Second Leeds)
(Bantam Battalion)*

18th Battalion
Highland Light Infantry
*(Fourth Glasgow)
(Bantam Battalion)*

19th Battalion
DurhamLight Infantry
*(Second County)
(Bantam Battalion)*

19th Battalion (Pioneers)
Northumberland Fusiliers
(Second Tyneside Pioneers)

36th (Ulster) Division

107 BRIGADE

8th Battalion
Royal Irish Rifles
(East Belfast)

9th Battalion
Royal Irish Rifles
(West Belfast)

10th Battalion
Royal Irish Rifles
(South Belfast)

15th Battalion
Royal Irish Rifles
(North Belfast)

108 BRIGADE

9th Battalion
**Princess Victoria's
(Royal Irish Fusiliers)**
(County Armagh)

11th Battalion
Royal Irish Rifles
(South Antrim)

12th Battalion
Royal Irish Rifles
(Central Antrim)

13th Battalion
Royal Irish Rifles
(First County Down)

109 BRIGADE

9th Battalion
**Royal Inniskilling
Fusiliers**
(County Tyrone)

10th Battalion
**Royal Inniskilling
Fusiliers**
(Derry)

11th Battalion
**Royal Inniskilling
Fusiliers**
(Donegal & Fermanagh)

14th Battalion
Royal Irish Rifles
(Young Citizens)

16th Battalion (Pioneers)
Royal Irish Rifles
(County Down Pioneers)

38th (Welsh)  Division

113 BRIGADE

13th Battalion
Royal Welsh Fusiliers
(First North Wales)

14th Battalion
Royal Welsh Fusiliers

15th Battalion
Royal Welsh Fusiliers
(First London Welsh)

16th Battalion
Royal Welsh Fusiliers

114 BRIGADE

10th Battalion
Welsh Regiment
(First Rhondda)

13th Battalion
Welsh Regiment
(Second Rhondda)

14th Battalion
Welsh Regiment
(Swansea Pals)

15th Battalion
Welsh Regiment
(Carmarthenshire)

115 BRIGADE

16th Battalion
Welsh Regiment
(Cardiff Pals)

10th Battalion
South Wales Borderers
(First Gwent Pals)

11th Battalion
South Wales Borderers
(Second Gwent Pals)

17th Battalion
Royal Welsh Fusiliers

19th Battalion (Pioneers)
Welsh Regiment
(Glamorgan Pioneers)

39th Infantry Division

116 BRIGADE

11th Battalion
Royal Sussex Regt
(First South Down)

12th Battalion
Royal Sussex Regt
(Second South Down)

13th Battalion
Royal Sussex Regt
(Third South Down)

14th Battalion
Hampshire Regt
(First Portsmouth)

117 BRIGADE

16th Battalion
**Rifle Brigade
(The Prince
Consort's Own)**
(St Pancras)

16th Battalion
**Sherwood Foresters
(Nottinghamshire &
Derbyshire Regt)**
(Chatsworth Rifles)

17th Battalion
**Sherwood Foresters
(Nottinghamshire &
Derbyshire Regt)**
(Welbeck Rangers)

17th Battalion
King's Royal Rifle Corps
(British Empire League)

118 BRIGADE

1/1st Battalion
Cambridgeshire Regt
(Territorial Force)

1/1st Battalion
Hertfordshire Regt
(Territorial Force)

1/6th Battalion
Cheshire Regiment
(Territorial Force)

4th/5th Battalion
**Black Watch (Royal
Highlanders)**
(Territorial Force)

13th Battalion (Pioneers)
Gloucestershire Regt
(Forest of Dean Pioneers)

16co06 A British gun crew preparing to fire an 8-inch howitzer.

16co04 An Australian gun crew loading a 9.2-inch siege howitzer during the fighting at Pozières.

16co03 The BL 8-inch howitzer Mark I, a British improvisation developed to provide heavy artillery. It used shortened and bored-out barrels from various redundant naval 6-inch guns. It remained in use on the Western Front throughout the war.

16co05 An Australian 18-pounder gun crew during the Battle of Pozières Ridge, Battle of the Somme 1916.

16co08 Men of the 16th Battalion, Middlesex Regiment, at the entrance to the 'White City' equipment dump, June 1916, before the Battle of the Somme.

16co11 British Vickers Machine Gun team, wearing early, crude gas protectors.

16co07 Priming mortar bombs – men of the King's Own Yorkshire Light Infantry.

16co12 A Lewis gun team wearing box respirators, issued to British troops in April 1916.

16co09 A fatgue detail of the Royal Irish Rifles behind the front line, Somme 1916.

16co15 A support trench with men of 86 Brigade waiting to attack on the morning of 1 July, 1916.

16co10 Men of the 1st Battalion Lancashire Fusiliers preparing to attack.

16co13, 16co16. British infantry leaving their trenches to walk across No Man's Land towards the German trenches on the morning of 1 July, 1916.

16co17 The Tyneside Irish, (Northumberland Fusiliers); men of 103 Brigade advancing in regular lines on the morning of 1 July, 1916.

16co18 As men of the first wave of the Tyneside Irish are swallowed up in the morning mist, whilst men of the second wave leave their trenches to follow on.

16co14 Two wounded men in the sunken road between Auchonvillers and Beaumont Hamel crawling back to their own line. This road had been ranged with great accuracy by German artillery. Many men of 86 Brigade were killed here on the morning of the attack, 1 July 1916.

16co28, 16co23, By mid morning on the day of the British attack, the Advanced Dressing Stations and Walking Wounded Collection Points became clogged with wounded men, which clearly indicated the enormity of the failure being experienced by the British Army as Haig's Big Push got underway.

16co20 Collecting Army Pay Books, private effects and identification discs from the dead. These men were cut down by German machine-gun fire.

16co19, 16co21, 16co33 British wounded being brought into the Advanced Dressing Station at Auchonvilliers. This work carried on for the next few days. From here the wounded were transported to the Main Dressing Stations. There were two Advanced Operating Centres for the opening stages of the Somme and six Casualty Clearing Stations where amulances could operate safely out of range of the German guns.

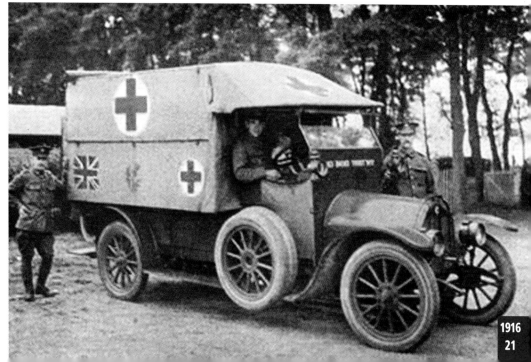

16co24 Roll Call for these men of a company of the 1st Battalion Lancashire Fusiliers, the survivors, on the morning of their failed attack.

16co27 Walking wounded, their injuries dressed at an Advanced Dressing Station, making their way to a Collection Point.
16co22 Preparing for a possible German counter attack.

16co29 Canadians with the new weapon for the Battle of Flers-Courcelette. The soldiers were no doubt wondering what sort of a show the 'tank' would perform in the coming attack on the German positions.

16co26 A trench captured by the 11th Battalion Cheshire Regiment at Ovillers-la-Boisselle. A sentry keeps watch while others sleep; note that the trench has been reveresed, with a new fire step roughly hacked out. Compare this with the well constructed German fire step opposite.

16co25 Troops moving up to the front passing alongside Mametz Wood.

16co32, 16co31 A new weapon for the infantry was introduced in 1916 – the Lewis gun. The automatic firing weapon was much lighter and less cumbersome than both the Maxim and Vickers machine guns, making it easier to move from one position to another quickly. However, it did cost more to manufacture.

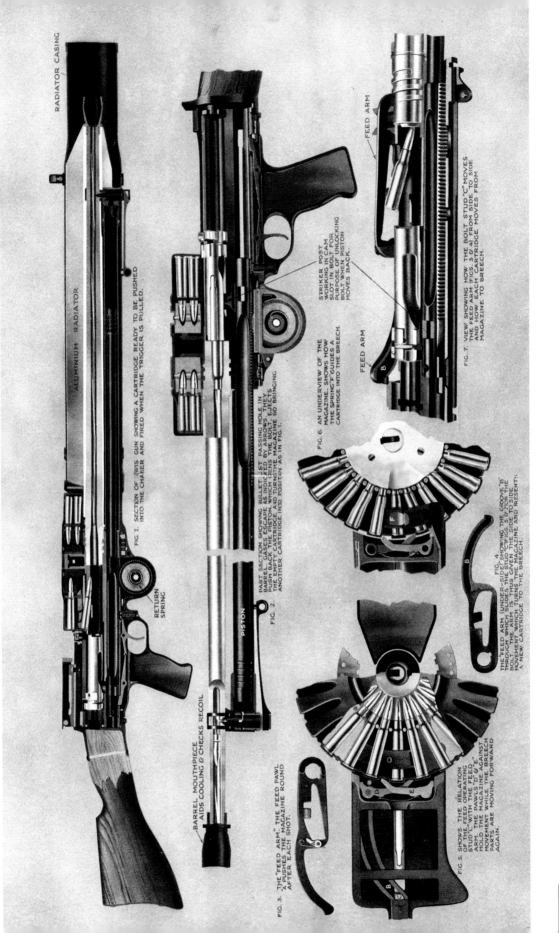

RADIATOR CASING

ALUMINIUM RADIATOR

RETURN SPRING

FIG. I. SECTION OF LEWIS GUN SHOWING A CARTRIDGE READY TO BE PUSHED INTO THE CHAMBER AND FIRED WHEN THE TRIGGER IS PULLED.

BARREL MOUTHPIECE AIDS COOLING & CHECKS RECOIL

PISTON

PART SECTION SHOWING BULLET JUST PASSING HOLE IN BARREL. THE EMPTY CASE (LEFT) IS INDICATED. THE BOLT IS HELD BACK WHILE THE PISTON MOVES BACK AND EJECTS THE EMPTY CARTRIDGE, AND TURNS THE MAGAZINE SO BRINGING ANOTHER CARTRIDGE INTO POSITION AS IN FIG.1.

FIG. 2.

FIG. 3. THE "FEED PAWL" A PUSHES THE MAGAZINE ROUND AFTER EACH SHOT.

FEED ARM

FIG. 7. VIEW SHOWING HOW THE BOLT STUD "C" MOVES THE FEED ARM (FIGS. 3 & 4) FROM SIDE TO SIDE AND HOW EACH CARTRIDGE MOVES FROM MAGAZINE TO BREECH.

STRIKER POST WORKING IN CAM SLOT IN BOLT FOR PURPOSE OF UNLOCKING BOLT WHEN PISTON MOVES BACK.

FEED ARM

FIG. 6. AN UNDERVIEW OF THE MAGAZINE. SHOWS HOW THE SPRING "F" GUIDES A CARTRIDGE INTO THE BREECH.

FIG. 4.

THE "FEED ARM (UNDER-SIDE) SHOWING THE GROOVE "B" THROUGH WHICH SLIDES THE STUD "C" (FIGS. 5 & 7) ON THE BOLT. THE ARM IS THUS GIVEN THE SIDE TO SIDE MOVEMENT WHICH TURNS THE MAGAZINE AND PRESENTS A NEW CARTRIDGE TO THE BREECH.

FIG. 5. SHOWS THE RELATION OF THE FEED OPERATING STUD "C" WITH THE FEED ARM. THE PAWLS D & E HELD BY SPRINGS AGAINST MAGAZINE WHILE THE BREECH PARTS ARE MOVING FORWARD AGAIN.

1916
28

Verdun

16co36 A fine example of a *poilu* (Warrior) – the French term for a Tommy.

16co41 Fort Vaux: months of fierce fighting and bombardment had pounded the concrete until it resembled natural rock..

Early French colour photographs of troops at Verdun in the summer of 1916.

16co39 French artillery officers observing German troop movements from Côte 304 (Hill 304).

16co40 Verdun, battered but undefeated.

16co42 A German machine gun captured in working order at one of the forts. It Most likely came from Fort Douaumont, as the Germans withdrew in good order from Fort Vaux and thoroughly demolished facilities, weapons and gun positions.

16GW884 Little had changed since the days of Nelson: some British crew members during a leisure period. Card games are going on as one reads the popular periodical *John Bull*.

16GW887 British naval officers in a crowded officers mess aboard a battleship. Note the officer lighting a cigar from a suspended naked light source for lighting cigarettes and cigars.

16GW885, 16GW886 British naval officers pictured at play on board a British battleship. The costumes range from a Georgian dandy, a medieval lord to a blacked-up indian and oriental. John Bull, almost certainly, maybe a Czar Nicholas and could that be Rasputin?

16GW888 Coaling a warship at sea – it was regarded by all on board to be the worst of all jobs. Here, loose coal is being bagged from the hold of the coaling ship and then hoisted aboard the battleship, where men wait to trolley the bags to chutes; bags are then emptied into the ship's bunkers and the sacks returned to the coaler for re-use. Once loaded, coal had to be continuously moved to ensure bunkers nearest the boilers were always full should power be suddenly needed. These problems were sufficiently serious for the Royal Navy to build HMS *Queen Elizabeth* in 1913 as an oil powered ship.

16GW889, 16GW890 Coal dust everywhere! Scrubbing upper and lower decks decks of a Royal Navy battleship following the dreaded coaling operation.

16GW891 Stoking the fires from coal bunkers close to the warship's boilers. Should the captain require speed from the engines.

16GW892 Raking ashes from the boilers on a battleship.

16GW893 A ship's engineer and warrant officer in an engine room overseeing the steam driven engines of a warship.

16GW894 A Roman Catholic priest says mass for sailors, possibly petitioning the Almighty for success in the coming battles.

16GW854, 16GW852 Officers and men on HMS *Iron Duke* were assured by the Bishop of London that God was with the men and vessels of the Grand Fleet. Many must have wondered how divine favour would be demonstrated in order to protect them and confound the foe in the coming fight.

16GW895 Secondary armament of a British battleship being readied for firing.

16GW896 A Royal Navy 'pom-pom' crew prepare for action. The pom-pom fired a shell one pound in weight over 3,000 yards. It was belt-fed from a 25-round fabric belt.

16GW853 The Bishop and Admiral Jellicoe, in conversation, after the Church Parade service.

16GW897 The Grand Fleet at sea.

16GW898 The Grand Fleet steaming ahead in columns.

The Grand Fleet had a total of thirty-two Dreadnought battleships available to use by the time of Jutland. Of these, twenty-eight took part, organized into four Battle Squadrons.

The twenty-four vessels of 2nd, 4th and 1st Battle Squadrons formed the main body of the battle fleet; they are listed from van to rear following their deployment to engage the German fleet, which was heading into the North Sea – 31 May 1916.

16GW899, 16GW900 Admiral John Jellicoe sallied forth to meet the German High Seas Fleet at the head of the 3rd Division of the 4th Battle Squadron. His Flagship was HMS *Iron Duke*, Captain Frederick Charles Dreyer.

16GW900 Heading the Royal Navy fleet was the 1st Division of the 2nd Battle Squadron with HMS *King George V* in the van under Captain Frederick Field.

16GW901 HMS *Ajax*,1st Division of the 2nd Battle Squadron. Captain George Henry Baird.

16GW903 HMS *Erin*,1st Division of the 2nd Battle Squadron. Captain the Hon Victor Albert Stanley.

16GW904 HMS *Centurion*,1st Division of the 2nd Battle Squadron. Captain Michael Culme-Seymour.

16GW910 Vice-Admiral Thomas Jerram, commanding the 1st Division.

16GW911 Rear- Admiral Arthur Leveson, commanding the 2nd Division.

16GW912 HMS *Orion*, (flagship), Captain Oliver Backhouse.

16GW913 HMS *Monarch* sailing down the River Tyne after her launching in 1911. She was Orion class, with 13.5 inch guns instead of the usual 12 inch. Captain George Borrett in command.

16GW914 HMS *Thunderer*, Orion class. Captain Andrew Fergusson in command.

16GW915 HMS *Conqueror*, Orion class. Captain Henry Tothill in command.

16GW916 Commanding the 4th Battle Squadron (Battleships) and the 4th Division, Vice-Admiral Sir Frederick Doveton Sturdee.

16GW917 HMS *Benbow* (flagship), Iron Duke class, commanded by Captain Henry Wise Parker.

16GW918 HMS *Bellerophon*, Iron Duke class, commanded by Edward Francis Bruen.

16GW919 HMS *Temeraire*, Iron Duke class, commanded by Edwin Veale Underhill.

16GW920 HMS *Vanguard*, Iron Duke class, commanded by James Douglas Dick.

16GW921 Rear Admiral Sir Alexander Ludovic Duff. Commanding 3rd Division of the 4th Battle Squadron.

16GW922 HMS *Superb* (flagship), 3rd Division, 4th Battle Squadron. Commanded by Captain Edmund Hyde Parker.

16GW924 HMS *Royal Oak*, 3rd Division, 4th Battle Squadron. Commanded by Captain Crawford Maclachlan.

16GW923 HMS *Canada*, 3rd Division, 4th Battle Squadron. Commanded by Captain Coldingham Masters Nicholson.

16GW925 Vice-Admiral Sir Cecil Burney, commanding 1st Battle Squadron (Battleships) and the 6th Division.

16GW926 HMS *Marlborough* (flagship), 6th Division, 1st Battle Squadron.

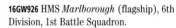

16GW927 HMS *Colossus* (flagship), 5th Division, 1st Battle Squadron. Captain Alfred Rogers Pound.

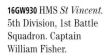

16GW928 Rear-Admiral Ernest Frederick Augustus Gaunt, commanding 5th Division, 1st Battle Squadron.

16GW929 HMS *Collingwood* 5th Division, 1st Battle Squadron. Captain James Clement Ley.

16GW930 HMS *St Vincent.* 5th Division, 1st Battle Squadron. Captain William Fisher.

16GW931 HMS *Neptune*. 5th Division, 1st Battle Squadron. Captain Gerald Bernard.

16GW932 HMS *Barham* (flagship). 6th Division of the 1st Battle Squadron (Battleships). Captain Arthur William Craig. Taking on coal.

16GW933 HMS *Valiant*. 6th Division of the 1st Battle Squadron (Battleships). Captain Maurice Woollcombe.

16GW934 HMS *Warspite*. 6th Division of the 1st Battle Squadron (Battleships). Captain Edward Phillpotts.

16GW935 HMS *Malaya*. 6th Division of the 1st Battle Squadron (Battleships). Captain the Hon. Algernon Douglas Harry Boyle.

16GW936 Rear-Admiral Sir Robert Keith Arbuthnot, commanding 1st Cruiser Squadron (Armoured Cruisers).

Two squadrons of Armoured Cruisers and one squadron of Light Cruisers were attached to the main body of the Grand Fleet to act as a scouting force.

16GW937 HMS *Defence* (flagship). Captain Stanley Venn Ellis.

16GW938 HMS *Warrior*. Captain Vincent Barkly Molteno.

16GW939 HMS *Duke of Edinburgh*. Captain Henry Blackett.

16GW940 HMS *Black Prince*. Captain Thomas Parry Bonham.

16GW941 HMS *Minotaur* (flagship). Captain Arthur Cloudesley Shovel Hughes D'Aeth. 2nd Cruiser Squadron.

16GW942 HMS *Shannon*. Captain John Saumarez Dumaresq.

16GW943 HMS *Cochrane*. Captain Eustace La Trobe Leatham.

16GW944, 16GW945 HMS *Hampshire*. Captain Herbert John Savill. After the Battle of Jutland the *Hampshire* sailed to Russia, carrying the Secretary of State for War, Field Marshal Lord Kitchener. She struck a mine and 15 minutes after the explosion she sank by the bow. Of the 655 crewmen and seven passengers aboard, only twelve crewmen managed to reach the shore alive; Kitchener and his staff were lost, along with the captain, John Savill.

16GW946 HMS *Comus*. Captain Alan Geoffrey Hotham. 4th Light Cruiser Squadron.
16GW947 HMS *Royalist*. 4th Light Cruiser Squadron. Captain the Hon. Herbert Meade.

16GW948 HMS *Calliope*, Commodore Le Mesurier, commanding the 4th Light Cruiser Squadron.

16GW949 HMS *Constance*. 4th Light Cruiser Squadron. Captain Cyril Samuel Townsend.

16GW950 HMS *Caroline*. 4th Light Cruiser Squadron. Captain Henry Ralph Crooke.

16GW951 HMS *Boadicea*, (attached to the 2nd Battle.Squadron for repeating visual signalling by fleet flag ships). Captain Louis Charles Stirling Woollcombe.

16GW952 HMS *Blanche* (attached to the 4th Battle Squadron on communication duties). Captain John Moore Casement.

16GW953 HMS *Active* (attached to Fleet Flagship for signalling tasks). Captain Percy Withers.

16GW954 HMS *Bellona* on signalling tasks (attached to the 1st Battle Squadron). Captain Arthur Brandreth Scott Dutton.

Two ships under the direct command of the Commander-in-Chief of the Grand Fleet.

16GW955 HMS *Abdiel* (minelayer). Commander Berwick Curtis.

16GW956 HMS *Oak* (destroyer). Lieutenant Commander Douglas Faviell.

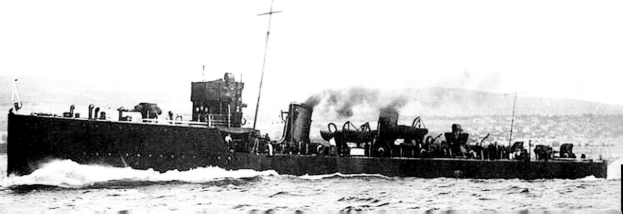

16GW957 Vice-Admiral
Sir David Richard Beatty.

16GW958 Battlecruiser Fleet Flagship: HMS *Lion*. Captain Alfred Ernle Montacute Chatfield.

16GW959 1st Battlecruiser Squadron: Rear-Admiral Osmond de Beauvoir Brock.

16GW960 HMS *Princess Royal* (flagship). Captain Walter Henry Cowan.

16GW961 HMS *Queen Mary*. Captain Cecil Irby Prowse.

16GW962 HMS *Tiger*. Captain Henry Bertram Pelly.

Royal Navy Battle Cruiser Fleet
This was a fleet of fast ships
operating independently and
ahead of the Grand Fleet. Its role
was to reconnoitre and engage
the scouting cruisers of the
German High Seas Fleet. Its main
force comprised six
battlecruisers, which were
supported by thirteen light
cruisers and eighteen destroyers.
Also, a new innovation and
novelty for the Royal Navy, an
early aircraft carrier – HMS
Engadine. The Battle Cruiser
Fleet, under the command of
Vice-Admiral Sir David Richard
Beatty, was subordinate to the
Commander in Chief of the Grand
Fleet, Admiral Jellicoe, but
operated independently.

16GW964 HMS *Indefatigable*, 2nd Battlecruiser Squadron. Captain Charles Sowerby.

16GW965 HMS *New Zealand* (flagship), 2nd Battlecruiser Squadron. Captain John Ernest Green.

16GW963 Rear-Admiral William Christopher Pakenham, commanding the 2nd Battlecruiser Squadron.

16GW966 Commodore Edwyn
Alexander-Sinclair, commanding
the 1st Light Cruiser Squadron.

16GW967 HMS *Galatea*.
Commodore Alexander-Sinclair.

16GW968 HMS *Phaeton*. Captain
John Ewen Cameron.

16GW969 HMS *Cordelia*. Captain
Tufton Percy Hamilton Beamish.

16GW970 HMS *Inconstant*.
Captain Bertram Sackville
Thesiger.

16GW971 HMS *Southampton*. Commodore Goodenough, seen with the 2nd Light Cruiser Squadron at full steam.

16GW976 Commodore William Goodenough, commanding the 2nd Light Cruiser Squadron.

16GW972 HMS *Birmingham*. Captain Arthur Allan Morison Duff.

16GW974 HMS *Nottingham*. Captain Charles Blois Miller.

16GW975 HMS *Dublin*. Captain Albert Charles Scott.

16GW977 HMS *Falmouth* (flagship). Captain John Douglas Edwards.

16GW978 HMS *Yarmouth*. Captain Thomas Drummond Pratt.

16GW979 HMS *Birkenhead*. Captain Edward Reeves.

16GW980 HMS *Gloucester*. Captain William Frederick Blunt.

16GW981 HMS *Engadine* (seaplane tender). Lieutenant-Commander Charles Robinson.

16GW983, 16GW984, 16GW985 A Royal Navy Short 184 seaplane landing; being made secure and winched aboard the tender vessel.

The SS *Engadine* had been a cross-Channel ferry and on the outbreak of war was converted into a tender and later fitted with hangars for four seaplanes. She would be employed in aerial reconnaissance work and bombing duties in the North Sea. In 1915 the Engadine was transferred to the Battlecruiser Fleet and, at Jutland, would fly the first ever heavier-than-air reconnaissance mission during a naval battle.

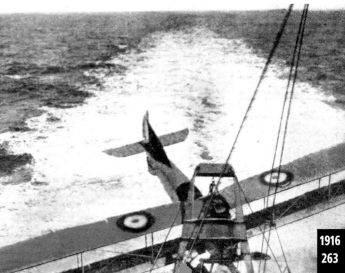

The German High Seas Fleet's reason for venturing into the North Sea was to lure the British ships into a trap, plotting to destroy a significant portion of the Grand Fleet. Making for an almighty clash of giants, the strategy pursued by the Royal Navy was to seek any opportunity to engage and at least cripple the German High Seas Fleet in battle. The British learned from signal intercepts that a major German fleet operation was imminent. On 30 May 1916, Admiral Jellicoe sailed with the Grand Fleet to rendezvous with Beatty's battle cruiser squadrons.

Opening moves were made by Vice-Admiral Franz Hipper's scouting group of five modern battlecruisers. They sailed at speed towards British controlled waters to provoke Vice-Admiral Sir David Beatty's battlecruiser squadrons to venture out and into the path of the German main force battleships.

On 31 May, Beatty encountered Hipper's fast battlecruisers and a running fight ensued, Hipper successfully drawing Beatty towards the German main force. When Beatty sighted the larger force and turned back, it was too late for two of his ships, which were sunk, from his total force of six battlecruisers and four battleships. The battleships, commanded by Rear-Admiral Sir Hugh Evan-Thomas,

formed a rearguard as Beatty withdrew. It was the turn of the German fleet to steam in hot pursuit towards Jellicoe's advanceing Grand Fleet.

With daylight fast fading, the two fleets, totalling 250 ships altogether, came within firing range for the biggest naval battle in history. In that initial engagement fourteen British ships were sunk against eleven German ships.

Throughout the night, Jellicoe manoeuvred to try and cut off the German High Seas Fleet from its bases, However, under the cover of darkness, Admiral Scheer broke through the British light forces forming the rearguard of the Grand Fleet and returned to port. It would not venture out again for the remainder of the war.

Both sides claimed victory. The British lost more ships and twice as many sailors. The British public, expecting the repeat of Trafalgar and the heady victories of Nelson, criticised Jellicoe's failure to force a decisive outcome. However, despite the Kaiser claiming a glorious victory for his High Seas Fleet, the plan of his admirals to destroy a significant part of the Royal Navy had failed and his High Seas Fleet remained in harbour for the rest of the war.

16GW986 Battlecruisers of Admiral Beatty's scouting force.

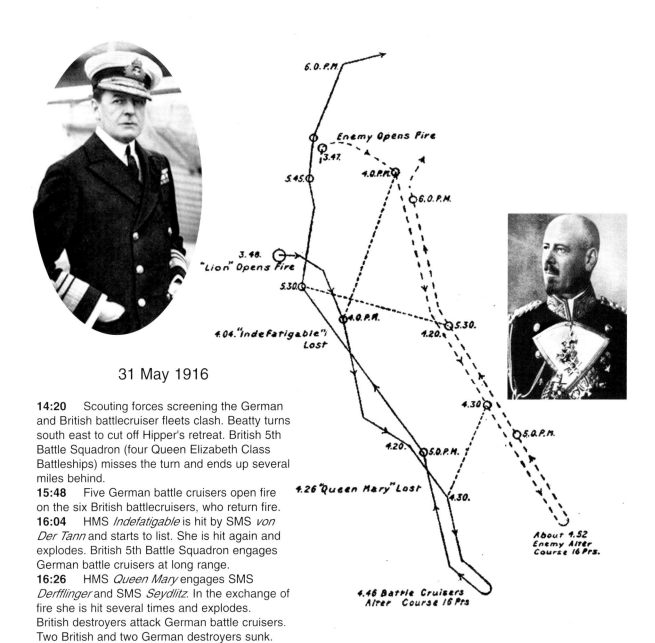

31 May 1916

14:20 Scouting forces screening the German and British battlecruiser fleets clash. Beatty turns south east to cut off Hipper's retreat. British 5th Battle Squadron (four Queen Elizabeth Class Battleships) misses the turn and ends up several miles behind.

15:48 Five German battle cruisers open fire on the six British battlecruisers, who return fire.

16:04 HMS *Indefatigable* is hit by SMS *von Der Tann* and starts to list. She is hit again and explodes. British 5th Battle Squadron engages German battle cruisers at long range.

16:26 HMS *Queen Mary* engages SMS *Derfflinger* and SMS *Seydlitz*. In the exchange of fire she is hit several times and explodes. British destroyers attack German battle cruisers. Two British and two German destroyers sunk.

16:38 Beatty sights the German High Seas Fleet, turns and runs north to draw the German Fleet to the Grand Fleet. The German battle-cruisers turn north to pursue. British 5th Battle Squadron forms a line in front of the High Seas Fleet to act as rearguard to the battlecruisers.

17:00 The British main force under Jellicoe is forty miles from the battlecruisers, approaching from the north-north-west.

The action between the two opposing forces of battlecruisers, 31 May 1916.

16GW989 Vice-Admiral Beatty on the bridge of his flagship, HMS *Lion*.
16GW990 Battlecruiser Fleet at full steam ahead in the North Sea: HMS *Tiger*, HMS *Lion* and HMS *Princess Royal*.

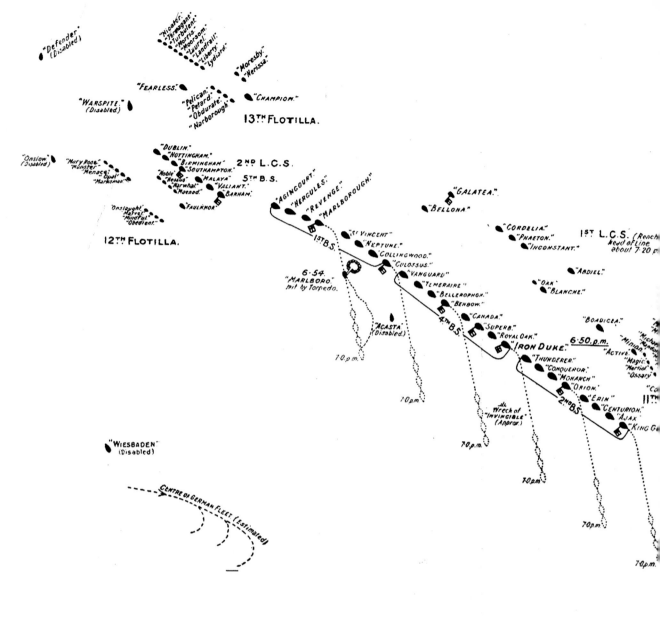

"Defender."
(Disabled)

"Nicator."
"Termagant."
"Turbulent."
"Moorsom."
"Morris."
"Laurel."
"Liberty."
"Lydiard."

"Moresby."
"Nerissa."

"Fearless."

"Warspite."
(Disabled)

"Pelican."
"Petard."
"Obdurate."
"Narborough."

"Champion."

13TH FLOTILLA.

"Onslow."
(Disabled)

"Mary Rose."
"Munster."
"Menace."
"Opal."
"Marksman."

"Dublin."
"Nottingham."
"Birmingham."
"Southampton."
"Noble."
"Nessus."
"Narwhal."
"Moorsod."
"Barham."

2ND L.C.S.

"Malaya."
"Valiant."

5TH B.S.

"Faulknor."

"Onslaught."
"Marvel."
"Mindful."
"Obedient."

12TH FLOTILLA.

"AGINCOURT."
"HERCULES."
"REVENGE."
"MARLBOROUGH."

1ST B.S.

"ST VINCENT."
"NEPTUNE."
"COLLINGWOOD."
"COLOSSUS."
"VANGUARD."
"TEMERAIRE."
"BELLEROPHON."
"BENBOW."
"CANADA."
"SUPERB."
"ROYAL OAK."

6.54.
"MARLBORO"
hit by Torpedo.

"GALATEA."
"BELLONA."

"CORDELIA."
"PHAETON."
"INCONSTANT."

1ST L.C.S. (Reach
head of line
about 7.20 p

"ARDIEL."

"OAK."
"BLANCHE."

"ACASTA."
(Disabled)

4TH B.S.

"BOADICEA."

6.50. p.m.

"MINION"
"Michael"
"Active."
"Magic."
"Martial."
"Ossory"

7.0 p.m.

"Wreck of
"INVINCIBLE"
(Approx.)

IRON DUKE.

"THUNDERER."
"CONQUEROR."
"MONARCH."
"ORION."
"ERIN."
"CENTURION."
"AJAX."
"KING G

2ND B.S.

11

7.0 p.m.

7.0 p.m.

7.0 p.m.

7.0 p.m.

7.0 p.m.

7.0 p.m.

"WIESBADEN"
(Disabled)

CENTRE OF GERMAN FLEET (Estimated)

16GW991 Shells falling among the British battlecruisers *Lion, Tiger, New Zealand, Queen Mary, Indefatigable* and *Princess Royal.*

"CHESTER."
"HAMPSHIRE."
"DUKE OF EDINBURGH."
"SHANNON."
CRUISERS. "COCHRANE"
"MINOTAUR."

Contest.
Fortune
Porpoise
Unity
Ophelia
Broke
TIPPERARY.

4TH FLOTILLA.

dent
scade
hates.

ng Star.
say.
"ROYALIST."
"CAROLINE."
"COMUS." 4TH L.C.S.
"CONSTANCE."
"CALLIOPE."

"INFLEXIBLE."
"INDOMITABLE."
"NEW ZEALAND."
"TIGER."
"PRINCESS ROYAL."
"LION."

"Hydra."
"Attack."
"Ariel."
"Acheron."
"Lizard."
"Lapwing."
"Goshawk."

BATTLE CRUISERS

"Christopher."
"Ophelia."
"CANTERBURY."

"GLOUCESTER."
"BIRKENHEAD."
3RD L.C.S. "YARMOUTH." 3RD L.C.S.
"FALMOUTH."

The Main Action

17:45   Admiral Hood's 3rd Battle Cruiser Squadron engages German cruisers attacking the light cruiser *Chester*. Hood's flagship, HMS *Invincible*, hits SMS *Wiesbaden*, which is unable to manoeuvre. The 1st Cruiser Squadron moves in to finish off the *Weisbaden* and is caught by the German battleships. HMS *Defence* is blown out of the water and HMS *Warrior* is disabled.

17:59   Destroyer HMS *Shark* is sunk.

18:00   The Grand Fleet begins to manouvre into line ahead formation.

18:20   HMS *Warspite's* rudder jams and she circles, drawing fire from the German High Seas Fleet. HMS *Warrior* limps away whilst the High Seas Fleet is distracted. Rear-Admiral Hood's battlecruisers join Beatty's force and attacks the German battlecruisers.

18:33   HMS *Invincible*, Hood's flagship, is hit by shells from SMS *Derfflinger* and explodes.

18:35   Sheer realises he is steaming towards the main British Battle Fleet. Just in time he orders a withdrawal. Jellicoe steams south to intercept and cut off the German High Seas Fleet

18:47   Hipper's flagship, SMS *Lutzow*, is disabled by hits from HMS *Invincible*.

18:55   Sheer orders another about turn to get back to his home base. He heads east-north-east and back at the British Grand Fleet.

19:00   Admiral Jellicoe's ships, invisible to Sheer in the dark, opens fire on the High Seas Fleet, silhouetted against the setting sun.

19:13   Sheer orders the German battlecruisers and torpedo boats to cover the retreat of the High Seas Fleet by attacking the Grand Fleet head on.

19:16   Sheer orders a third 'About turn' and escapes again.

20:30   Main action ends, with the final shots between the battle ships and battlecruisers.

Jellicoe elects to continue south-south-east to cut off Sheer from his base. Sheer actually cuts across Jellicoe's wake and takes a route towards Horn's Reef and then home

22:30   SMS *Frauenlob* sunk. HMS *Tipperary* sunk by German battleships.

1 June 1916 The Night Action

00:20   HMS *Ardent* and HMS *Fortune* sunk by German battleships. HMS *Black Prince* sunk by German battleships.

01:05   HMS *Turbulent* sunk by SMS *Westfalen*.

01:47   SMS *Lutzow* is scuttled.

02:00   SMS *Elbing* scuttled.

SMS *Pommern* torpedoed.

V4 explodes and sinks.

05:20   SMS *Ostfriesland* hits a mine laid by HMS *Abdiel*.

15:00   High Seas Fleet is back at anchor in Wilhelmshaven.

16GW992 HMS *Warspite* and HMS *Malaya* seen from HMS *Valiant* at 14:00 hrs on 31 May 1916.

16GW997, 16GW998 The British battlecruiser HMS *Indefatigable* sinking after being hit by shells from the German battlecruiser *Von Der Tann*. As she struggled out of the line she was hit by another salvo on the foredeck. In the resulting massive explosion all but two of *Indefatigable*'s crew of 1,119 were killed.

16GW993,16GW994 HMS *Queen Mary* was hit twice by the German battlecruisers SMS *Derfflinger* and *Seydlitz* and blew apart when her magazines exploded. 1,266 crewmen were lost; eighteen survivors were picked up by two British destroyers and German ship. Shells can be seen falling around HMS *Lion*. A similar fate was averted when a dying officer ordered the *Lion's* magazine to be flooded after a gun turret was hit.

16GW995 SMS *Derfflinger* firing a salvo from her eight 12-inch guns.

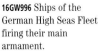

16GW996 Ships of the German High Seas Fleet firing their main armament.

16GW1002, 16GW1003, 16GW1004 Destruction of HMS *Invincible* photographed from HMS *Inflexible*. There were only six survivors; 1,026 men perished.

HMS *Invincible*, flagship of the 3rd Battlecruiser Squadron, was engaged by SMS *Lützow* and SMS *Derfflinger*. The two German ships fired three salvoes each at *Invincible* and sank her in just 90 seconds. One 12-inch shell from the third salvo struck her midships. The shell penetrated the front of a gun turret, blew off the roof and detonated the midships magazines, blowing the ship in half. Of her ship's complement 1,026 officers and men were killed, including Rear-Admiral Hood. There were only six survivors, picked up by HMS *Badger*. Two halves of the *Invincible* stuck up above the surface for a while, the broken ends resting on the sandy sea bottom.

16GW1006 Captain Arthur L. Cay, commanding HMS *Invincible*.

16GW1007 Rear-Admiral Horace Hood, commander of the 3rd Battlecruiser Squadron. Killed when his flagship, HMS *Invincible*, exploded.

16GW1008 HMS *Invincible,* flagship of the 3rd Battlecruiser Squadron during the Battle of Jutland. She was destroyed by a magazine explosion during the battle after 'Q' turret (mid-ship) was hit by a shell.

16GW1009 Royal Navy destroyers and battlecruisers steaming to engage the enemy.

16GW1010 At the height of the Battle of Jutland, Royal Navy destroyers acting as a screen against torpedo attack for the battlecruisers and battleships.

16GW1011 British battlecruisers in action at Jutland.

16GW2012 A German destroyer launches a torpedo during the Battle of Jutland.

16GW1054 Light Cruiser HMS *Royalist* was launched in January 1915 and assigned to the 4th Light Cruiser Squadron of the Grand Fleet. She took part in the Battle of Jutland.

16GW1056 Manning the main armament of an Arethusa class cruiser is the 6-inch naval gun.

16GW1057 The 4 inch Mk VII gun. It first appeared in 1914 as secondary armament on Arethusa class cruisers.

16GW1055 The Royal Navy''s most modern 6-inch naval gun when the First World War began. On the deck of HMS *Royalist*.

16GW1013, 16GW1014 The Royal Navy 2nd Battlecruiser Squadron sails into action at Jutland.

16GW1016 SMS *Schleswig-Holstein* firing her guns at Jutland. During the battle she only fired twenty shells. She was hit once by a shell on the port side that disabled one of her guns.

16GW1015 Stunned sailers aboard the destroyer HMS *Badger* prepare to pick up survivors from the *Invincible*.

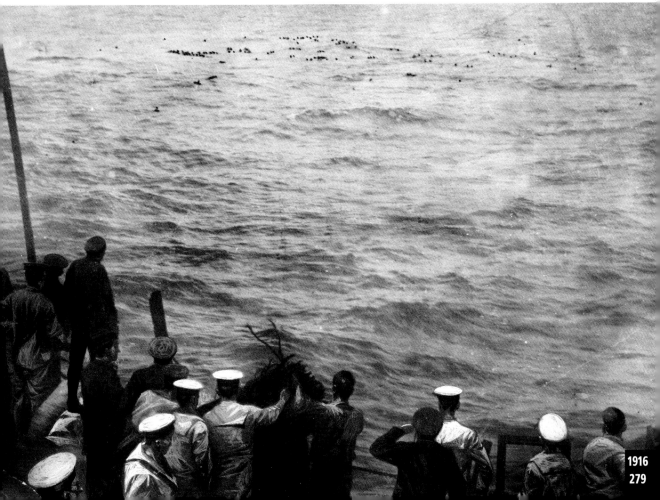

16GW1017 Shells falling around HMS *Lion* during the afternoon of 31 May 1916.

16GW1018 HMS *Lion* receives a direct hit

16GW1019 During the Battle of Jutland, HMS *Lion*, the flagship of Admiral Beatty's Battlecruiser Fleet, was hit twice within minutes by accurate firing from SMS *Lützow*. HMS *Lion* scored her first hit on the *Lützow* shortly afterwards. This was followed by the German cruiser scoring another hit, this time on one of the gun turrets. The shell exploded over the centre of the left-hand gun, killing or wounding the turret gun crew. A fire started and burned fiercely, with flames reaching as high as the masthead. Most of the magazine and shell room crews, still in the lower part of the mounting, were killed. It is highly probable that the magazine would have exploded, destroying the ship, if it had not already been flooded. The turret commander, Royal Marine Major Francis Harvey, despite being mortally wounded, ordered the magazine flooded. He was posthumously awarded the Victoria Cross for having given that order despite the loss of both legs.

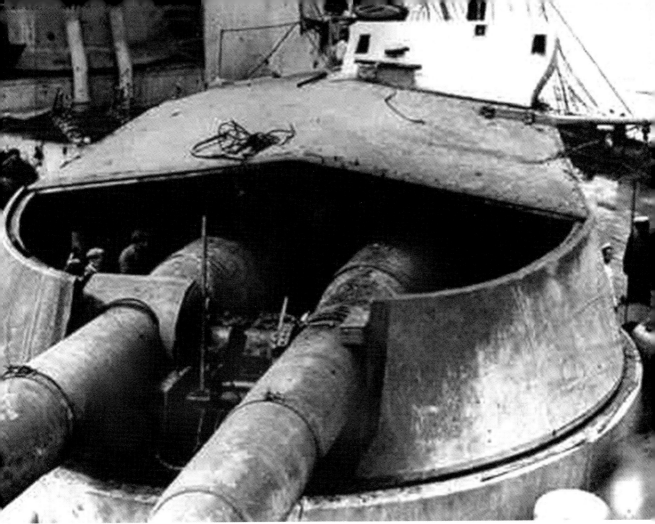

16GW1020 HMS *Lion's* midships 'Q' 13.5-inch turret after the Battle of Jutland, 1916. Only the prompt flooding of the magazine saved the ship from a catastrophic explosion.

16GW1021 Inside the turret of a Royal Navy gun casemate, with some of the ship's gun crew providing a comparison between the size of the breeches of the 13.5 inch-inch guns and the men operating the twin-mounted weapons. The noise, fumes and constant weapon recoils during an engagement with the enemy can be imagined. Add a blazing inferno from ignited charges caused by a direct hit and we have the conditions suffered by the crew of HMS *Lion*.

16GW1022 Mortally-wounded, Major Francis Harvey, of the Royal Marines, gave orders to flood the magazine which fed the turret with 13.5-inch shells. In doing so he ensured that the fire raging in the smashed turret did not reach the bowels of *Lion* and blow the ship apart – unlike HMS *Queen Mary*, HMS *Invincible* and HMS *Indefatigable*. The three battlecruisers blew apart when shells exploded their magazines after a hit on a gun casemate.

16GW1023 The battlecruiser HMS *Tiger* underway at speed during the battle. The ship was hit fifteen times by large calibre shells, killing twenty-four members of her crew and wounding a further forty-six.

16GW1024 Two sailors looking through a shell hole in the forward turret of the battlecruiser HMS *Tiger*.

Beatty sights the German main force of the High Seas Fleet, turns and runs north to draw the German Fleet to Jellicoe's force – the Grand Fleet. The German battlecruisers turn north to pursue. The British 5th Battle Squadron forms a line in front of the High Seas Fleet to act as rearguard to Beatty's battlecruisers.

16GW1025 Beatty's battlecruisers withdrawing.

16GW1026 Vice-Admiral Hugh Evan-Thomas, commanding the 5th Battle Squadron.

16GW1027 Ships of the 5th Battle Squadron during the run to the north and the screening of Beatty's battlecruisers.

16GW1028, 16GW1029 Where shells struck the battlecruiser HMS *Tiger*.

16GW1030 HMS *Barham*, flagship of Vice-Admiral Hugh Evan-Thomas.

16GW1031 Ships of the 3rd Battlecruiser Squadron at Jutland.

HMS *Chester* was one of the screening cruisers for the 3rd Battlecruiser Squadron; she encountered the German Second Scouting Group of four light cruisers, including the SMS *Wiesbaden*. In the exchange of fire HMS *Chester* was heavily damaged.

16GW1032 A Victoria's Cross was won by a sixteen year old boy, Jack Cornwell, when he stayed at his gun post awaiting orders after the entire gun crew was either killed or wounded.

16GW1033 Caption in a popular magazine of the day: Boy (First Class) J. Cornwell of the *Chester*, though mortally wounded stands at his post amid the dead and wounded gun crew.

16GW1034 The shielded 5.5-inch gun mounting where Cornwell was serving as a sight-setter was affected by at least four nearby hits.

16GW1035 At 4.51 pm, 31 May 1916, Jellicoe signaled the Admiralty that a 'Fleet Action is Imminent'.

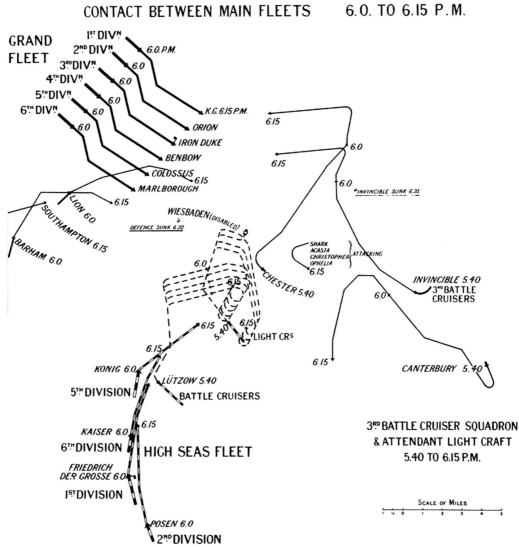

CONTACT BETWEEN MAIN FLEETS   6.0. TO 6.15 P.M.

GRAND
FLEET

1ᵀᴴ DIVᴺ
2ᴺᴰ DIVᴺ   6.0.P.M.
3ᴿᴰ DIVᴺ   6.0
4ᵀᴴ DIVᴺ   6.0
5ᵀᴴ DIVᴺ   6.0
6ᵀᴴ DIVᴺ   6.0
6.0

K.G. 6.15 P.M.
ORION
IRON DUKE
BENBOW
COLOSSUS   6.15
MARLBOROUGH

6.15
6.15
6.0
INVINCIBLE SUNK 6.35

LION 6.0   6.15
SOUTHAMPTON 6.15
BARHAM 6.0

WIESBADEN (DISABLED)
DEFENCE SUNK 6.20

SHARK
ACASTA
CHRISTOPHER   ATTACKING
OPHELIA
6.15

INVINCIBLE 5.40
3ᴿᴰ BATTLE
CRUISERS

6.0

CHESTER 5.40

6.0
6.15
6.15
5.40   LIGHT CRˢ

6.15
6.15

6.15
KONIG 6.0
5ᵀᴴ DIVISION

LÜTZOW 5.40
BATTLE CRUISERS

CANTERBURY 5.40

KAISER 6.0   6.15
6ᵀᴴ DIVISION   HIGH SEAS FLEET

FRIEDRICH
DER GROSSE 6.0
1ˢᵀ DIVISION

3ᴿᴰ BATTLE CRUISER SQUADRON
& ATTENDANT LIGHT CRAFT
5.40 TO 6.15 P.M.

POSEN 6.0
2ᴺᴰ DIVISION

SCALE OF MILES

16GW1037 HMS *Royal Oak*, HMS *Iron Duke*, HMS *Canada* and HMS *Superb* manouvreing at Jutland.

16GW1038 A Royal Navy battleship manouevring for a broadside.

16GW1039 A battleship of the Grand Fleet firing her main armament.

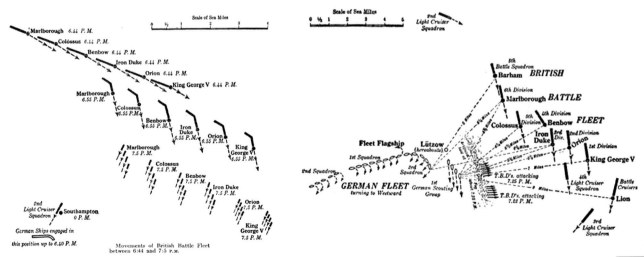

Movements of British Battle Fleet
between 6:44 and 7:5 P.M.

16GW1040 HMS *Hardy* leading a flotilla of torpedo-boat destroyers.

Battle of Jutland VC award.

On the afternoon of 31 May, 1916, Commander Jones in HMS *Shark*, a torpedo boat destroyer, led a division of destroyers to attack the enemy Battle Cruiser Squadron. In the course of this attack a shell hit the bridge of the *Shark*, and disabling the steering gear. Shortly afterwards another shell disabled the main engines, leaving the vessel helpless. Commander Jones, though wounded in the leg, went aft to help connect and man the after wheel. Meanwhile the fore-castle gun with its crew had been blown away, and the same fate soon afterwards befell the after gun and crew. Commander Jones then went to the midship and the only remaining gun, and personally assisted in keeping it in action. All this, time the *Shark* was subjected to very heavy fire from enemy light cruisers and destroyers at short range. The gun's crew of the midship gun was reduced to three, of whom an Able Seaman was soon badly wounded in the leg. A few minutes later Commander Jones was hit by a shell, which took off his leg above the knee, but he continued to give orders to his gun's crew, while a Chief Stoker improvised a tourniquet round his thigh. Noticing that the Ensign was not properly hoisted, he gave orders for another to be hoisted. Soon afterwards, seeing that the ship could not survive much longer, and as a German Destroyer was closing, he gave orders for the surviving members of the crew to put on lifebelts. Almost immediately after this order had been given, the *Shark* was struck by a torpedo and sank. Commander Jones, unfortunately, was not amongst the few survivors picked up by a neutral vessel during the night.

16GW1041 Commander Loftus William Jones, (killed in action) and awarded a posthumus Victoria Cross.

16GW1042 HMS *Shark*, under Commander Jones, led a squadron of destroyers in an attack on the German Battle Cruiser Squadron.

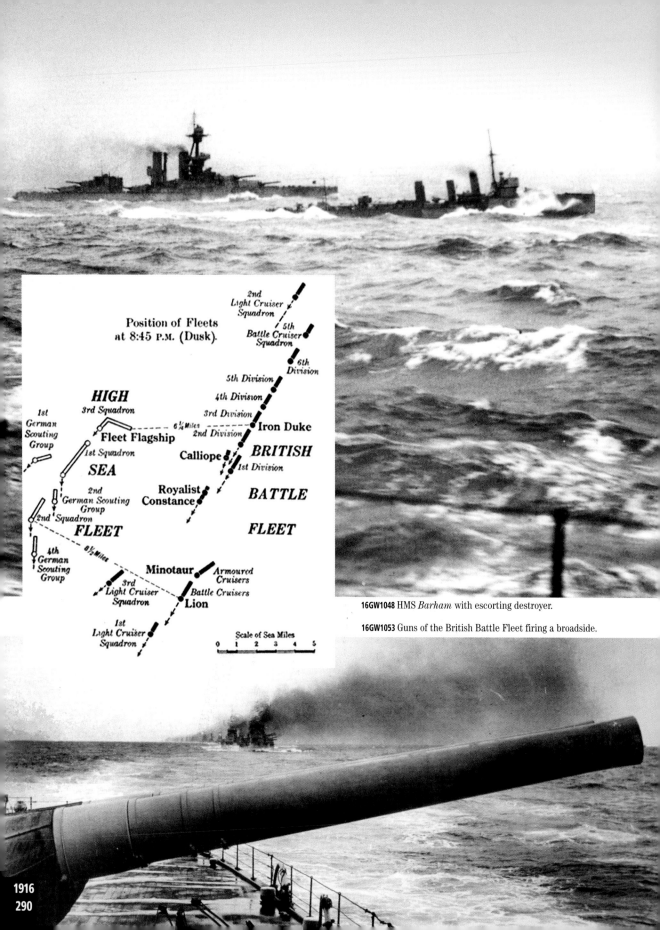

Position of Fleets at 8:45 P.M. (Dusk).

2nd Light Cruiser Squadron

5th Battle Cruiser Squadron

6th Division

5th Division

4th Division

3rd Division

Iron Duke

2nd Division

HIGH

3rd Squadron

1st German Scouting Group

Fleet Flagship

6¼ Miles

BRITISH

1st Squadron

Calliope

1st Division

SEA

2nd German Scouting Group

Royalist Constance

BATTLE

2nd Squadron

FLEET

4th German Scouting Group

8½ Miles

FLEET

Minotaur

Armoured Cruisers

3rd Light Cruiser Squadron

Battle Cruisers

Lion

1st Light Cruiser Squadron

Scale of Sea Miles

0 1 2 3 4 5

16GW1048 HMS *Barham* with escorting destroyer.

16GW1053 Guns of the British Battle Fleet firing a broadside.

16GW1049 The light cruiser HMS *Birmingham* suffered some splinter damage.

16GW1050 View from the bridge of a British battleship of the Grand Fleet.

16GW1052 SMS *Moltke* steaming back to the base at Wilhelmshaven, 1 June 1916, after the Battle of Jutland. Her stern is low in the water afte being hit four times. One shell passsed clean through from port to starboard.

16GW1044 SMS *Seydlitz*, severly battered and with her foredeck level with the water, managed to limp home after Jutland. *Kapitän zur See* von Egidy wrote his account of the action.

16GW1043 *Kapitän* Christoph Moritz von Egidy, commander of SMS *Seydlitz*.

The first hit we received was a 12-inch shell that struck Number Six, 6-inch gun casemate, on the starboard side, killing everybody except the Padre... Splinters perforated air leads in the compartment beneath and fumes entered the starboard main turbine compartment. The gunnery central station reported: 'No answer from C turret. Smoke and fumes pouring out of the voice pipes from C turret.' We lost only twenty dead. Only one turret was put out of action.

When Beatty turned to the north, we had a wonderful view of the British destroyer flotillas going full speed into the attack. They were intercepted by two of our flotillas, but we did not have much time to watch the outcome.

Our foretop reported first one, then more torpedo tracks in the water. We tried to avoid them by sharp turns, but finally one got us forward of the bridge.

'Steering failure!' called the helmsman and automatically shouted down from the armoured shaft to the control room: 'Steer from control room!'. We felt great relief when the red helm indicator responded. The first casualty on the bridge was a signal yeoman, who collapsed after a splinter had pierced his neck. Another signalman took over his headphone in addition to his own.

Visibility decreased and there seemed to be an endless line of ships ahead. But we saw only incessant flashes, mostly four discharges in the peculiar British 'rippling' salvoes way of firing. Our ship received hit after hit, but our guns remained silent because we could not make out any targets. The portside casemates were suffering heavy damage and a human chain had to be formed to pass ammunition from the lee battery. Suddenly, in B turret, there was a tremendous explosion followed by smoke, dust and general confusion. At the order 'Clear the Turret!' the gun crew evacuated, even using the traps for the empty shell cases. A shell had hit the front plate and a splinter of armour plate had ripped away,, killing the right-hand gunlayer.

The stokers and coal trimmers deserved the highest praise, for they had to wield their shovels mostly in the dark, often up to their knees in water. Unfortunately, we had very poor coal, which produced so much slag that the furnesses had to be cleaned constantly. Grates burnt through and fell into the ash-pits. Spare fire grates had to be fitted in the thick of the battle. Even the beams supporting the grates were bent by the intense heat.

Around 2000 hours we came under heavy fire, followed by a distinct lull during which, turrets could be opened and fresh air blown through the whole ship.

When we left the bridge we saw a frightful scene. One of the last shells had passed through the charthouse and burst in the lee of the bridge, killing or injuring my aide, his party of messengers and some signal ratings.

Darkness fell and we had to make preparations for the next morning, for we were sure to meet the British again. Searchlights were repaired, night recognition signals were rigged and ammunition carried to the undamaged guns. At first, we could continue to follow the battlecruiser SMS Moltke, but soon we had to slow down as water began to come over the forecastle as our bows settled. Steering was difficult, as was finding the right course, for the main gyro compartment was flooded and the after gyro unreliable. Its normal circuit had been destroyed, and the new connection short-circuited off and on. The shocks had made the magnetic compass entirely undependable. Sounding had its problems, too: the sounding machines in the casemates were reduced to scrap, while the hand-leads fouled the torn nets and then parted.

Our charts were covered with blood and the spare charts were inaccessible in a flooded compartment.

We made it back, arriving off Wilhelmshaven 3 June 1916, where we were welcomed by the crews of the battleships anchored there. The Seydlitz had been hit by twenty-one heavy shells and one torpedo; we lost ninety-eight men killed and fifty-five injured and had four heavy and two medium guns put out of action.

16GW1044 SMS *Seydlitz* smoking badly and heavily damage, having been hit twenty-one times by shells and one torpedo.

16GW1045 SMS *Seydlitz* with her bow low in the water and listing to port, struggles back to Wilhelmshaven.

16GW1058 SMS *Seydlitz* undergoing extensive repairs.

16GW1059 Where two British shells struck the *Seydlitz*.

16GW1060 The *Von der Tann* in Wilhelmshaven being repaired after the Battle of Jutland; a British 15-inch shell hole can be seen on the waterline.

16GW1061 Shell strikes on two gun turrets can be seen on the *Seydlitz,* also a hit in the side.

16GW1062 The second shell hit on C Turret of the *Seydlitz.*

16GW1063 Inside damage on the *Von der Tann.* Fighting on warships led to horrific injuries in the confined spaces, where hits shattered the metal plating, turning it into red hot shards .

16GW1000 Battle damage to SMS *Derfflinger*: pictured here undergoing extensive repairs in the shipyards at Wilhelmshaven.

16GW999 A gaping hole blown through the superstructure of the *Derfflinger*; the sailor gives some indication of the size of the hole torn in the ship.

16GW1001 SMS *Seydlitz*: a British 15-inch shell strike to a gun casemate killed most of the crew and wounded five; the bulkhead door has been rammed against the breech of the 15 cm gun

16GW1064 Admiral Beatty and his staff after the Battle of Jutland.

16GW1065 Q Turret of HMS *Lion* had its roof blown off during the battle. Its magazine was saved from exploding by the timely action of Major Francis Harvey of the Royal Marines, who gave orders to flood the magazine, thus saving the ship.

16GW1066 Kaiser Wilhelm II addressing officers of his High Seas Fleet after the Battle of Jutland: picture by Claus Bergen.

When the battle ended the British had lost three battlecruisers, three armoured cruisers and eight destroyers. Sailors and marines killed amounted to 6,094; wounded men numbered 674 men; 177 had been rescued from the sea and made prisoners of war.

The Germans had lost one battlecruiser, one pre-dreadnought cruiser, four light cruisers, and five destroyers. Men killed numbered 2,551, with 507 wounded. If based purely on losses, it was a German victory – it was hailed as such in Germany. The might of the Royal Navy, however, had not been seriously affected and stood ready, with twenty-two of her twenty-four battleships ready for combat. Losses were soon made good by the addition of three more super-dreadnoughts. The German fleet had run to port and safety with only eight of its sixteen dreadnoughts ready for further immediate action. It never sailed out again for the remainder of the war, thus it could be argued that Jutland was a British victory.

16GW1067 King George V, speaking from the deck of the badly damaged HMS *Warspite*, addressed a parade of sailors from the Grand Fleet after the Battle of Jutland.

The British and German people were persuaded to believe that the clash of the two opposing fleets had resulted in a great sea victory for their respective navies.

Chapter Five:

Battle of the Somme

With the Australians

16GW602,16GW704 Departure of some of the first troops to leave Australia from Sydney, 18 August 1914.

16GW601 Australian light horsemen. The soldiers are of the original contingent of the Australian Imperial Force and the photo was taken prior to their departure from Australia in November 1914. The soldier on the right is Trooper William Harry Rankin Woods,1st Light Horse Regiment, who died of wounds on 15 May 1915, one of the first light horsemen to die during the fighting at Gallipoli.

16GW605 On the quayside at Melbourne: departing troops, bound for the World War and adventure.

16GW604 Departure of troops from Hobart.

16GW603 Departure of a draft in 1915; news of casualties caused anxiety for those seeing their loved ones leave. Here a girl has broken into the ranks to cling on to her man. A policeman has to intervene to remove her gently but firmly.

16GW606 Sailing of the first Australian and New Zealand contingents for Europe. Thirty-six transports leaving King George's Sound, Western Australia, 1 November 1914. The photograph has been taken from HMT *Orvieto*, carrying Major General Bridges and the HQ of the 1st Australian Infantry Division.

16GW607 Infantry embarking at Melbourne, 18 October, 1914. Men of 2 Infantry Brigade waiting to go aboard HMT *Horarata* (left) and HMT *Benalla* (right).

16GW608 Men of the newly formed Australian divisions (the 4th and 5th Divisions) at the Suez Canal, 1916.

16GW611 Men of the 1st Infantry Battalion moving back to base from an advanced Suez Canal defence line, February 1916, prior to their leaving for France.

16GW612 Review of an Australian division early in 1916. The troops are marching past Lieutenant General Sir Archibald Murray at Tel el Kebir, Egypt.

16GW705 Lieutenant General Murray, commander of the British troops in Egypt, wrote to General Robertson, 18 March 1916, *'The Australians are, from a physical point of view, a magnificent body of men but have no idea of ordinary decency or self control'.*

16GW610 Australian soldiers among some French school children, 1916.

16GW609 The 1st and 2nd Divisions with the New Zealand Division (forming I Anzac Corps) arriving in France, Sunday 2 April 1916. Corps Commander, General Birdwood, addresses the men from the deck of HMT *Transylvania*.

16GW706 Corps Commander, Lieutenant General William Riddell Birdwood. In February 1916 the Australian and New Zealand contingents in Egypt, were reorganised to incorporate the reinforcements that had accumulated during the previous year: two corps were formed, I ANZAC Corps and II ANZAC Corps. I ANZAC Corps was the first to depart for France, Birdwood, in command.

16GW614 The Rt. Hon. W. M. Hughes and Lieutenant Colonel Watson, commanding the 24th Battalion, watching as the men march to their billets near Croix du Bac, south of Armentières, 1 June, 1916.

1916
310

16GW613 A battalion of 6 Brigade, newly arrived in Flanders, are showing off their recently issued steel helmets.

16GW615 A portion of a sand-bag breastwork in Flanders held by the New Zealand Division near Armentières, 7 June, 1916.

16GW616 New Zealand billets being shelled by the Germans.

16GW617 A view across No Man's Land from the line held by the Anzacs. 'Knife rests' holding barbed wire protect both German and Anzac frontline trenches. Soil is piled up along the front of the German trench line.

16GW618 A working party of the 11th Battalion coming out of the line, 3 June 1916, after working to repair dugouts. Note that they are walking alongside a narrow gauge railway track used to bring up supplies at night.

16GW620 Men working on a communication trench in Flanders. In this sector the 'trenches' consisted of breastworks raised above the level of the surrounding ground; this was because of the high water table.

16GW623 Before and after aerial photographs of one of the earliest trench raids made by the Australians, 12 June 1916. The raid was carried out by the 6th Battalion. The upper photograph shows No Man's Land and the two opposing lines on 5 May. The lower photograph was taken on 17 June and clearly shows the effects of the 'box' barrage laid down by the Australian artillery.

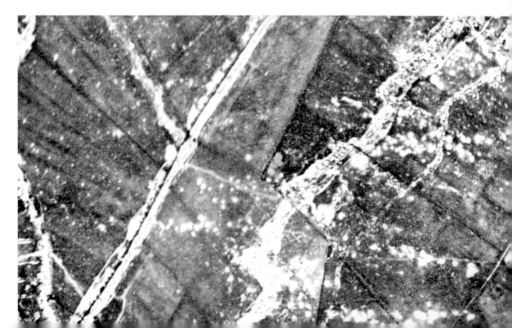

16GW619 A sector behind the lines between Estaire and Armentières. Men working alongside a barge on the River Lys.

16GW621 Crater made by a German minenwerfer exploding behind the front line trench of the 11th Battalion, 30 May 1916. The bombardment was in a short section of the line near Cordonnerie Farm and was in support of a German raid. In the bombardment forty men were killed and sixty wounded.

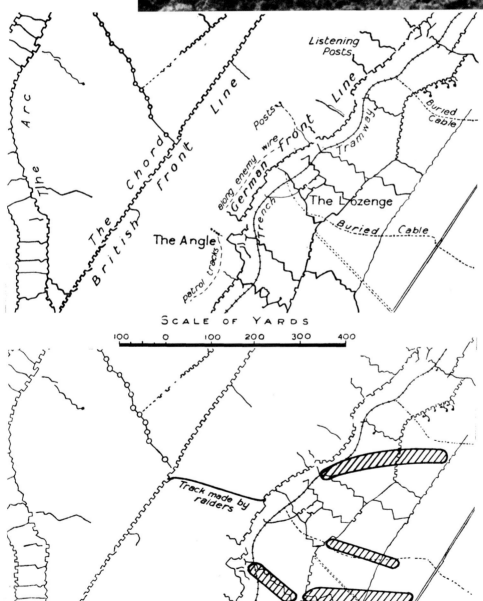

16GW622 Key to photographs on the opposite page. The shaded areas are the artillery targeted sections, the plan being to protect the raiders on three sides by a barrage of exploding shells.

16GW699 A fatigue party of 7 Brigade laden with sandbags passing 'Gibraltar', a bunker at Pozières, in late August. A house once stood here and the Germans fortified it – the concrete block protected a staircase leading to a cellar used as a headquarters. The height made it an excellent observation post.

16GW710 Australian machine gunners returning from the trenches at Pozières; passing 'Casualty Corner', near Contalmaison. A working party is heading in the opposite direction, up to the line.

16GW711 An 18-pounder gun crew during the Battle of Pozières Ridge.

16GW713 Drawing water for the gun crews.

16GW712 An Australian gun crew loading a 9.2-inch Siege howitzer during the fighting at Pozières.

16GW714 Men of the 1st Anzac Division wearing captured headgear strike a pose depicting German surrender after successful fighting at Pozières.

16GW720 King George V and Prince Edward at the Somme Front with General Rawlinson and Staff officers.

16GW626 5th Australian Division's Advanced Headquarters, several hundred yards from the front line at Fleurbaix, shortly before the move to the Somme. The mess and orderly room were in a sandbag shelter and the cook house was in farm buildings to the rear. This was a quiet sector of the Western Front.

16GW625 King George V, with Haig, along with some of the staff of the 5th Australian Division at the Infantry School near Sailly-sur-la-Lys, July 1916. The 5th Division had just arrived on the Somme.

16GW624 Men of the 12th Battalion resting in the village of Naours on their way to the Somme front, 12 July 1916. The 1st, 2nd and 4th Australian Divisions were moving up to take part in the Franco-British offensive which had begun on the 1 July.

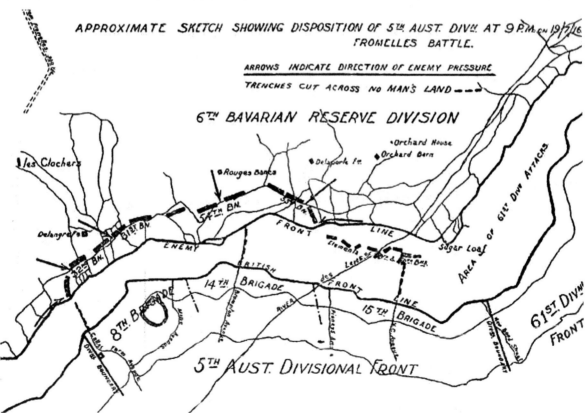

APPROXIMATE SKETCH SHOWING DISPOSITION OF 5TH. AUST. DIVN. AT 9 P.M. ON 19/7/16
FROMELLES BATTLE.

ARROWS INDICATE DIRECTION OF ENEMY PRESSURE
TRENCHES CUT ACROSS NO MAN'S LAND ---→

6TH BAVARIAN RESERVE DIVISION

Orchard House

les Clochers
Rouges Bancs
Delaporte Fm.
Orchard Barn

54TH BN.
57TH BN.

Delangre
53RD BN.
FRONT LINE
Area of 61ST Divn ATTACKS

Sugar Loaf

ENEMY
52ND BN.
Elements of
Left of 60TH & 59TH BN.

BRITISH

8TH BRIGADE
14TH BRIGADE
FRONT
LINE
15TH BRIGADE
61ST DIVN
FRONT

5TH AUST. DIVISIONAL FRONT

1916
322

16GW627 The battlefield of Fromelles, a photograph taken many months after the fighting. The 5th Australian Division and the British 61st Division attacked this part of the German line on 19 July. This area was covered by men of 15 Brigade (5th Australin Division) advancing towards the camera. In the middle distance is the channel of a brook, the des Layes, in which many men were killed by machine-gun fire.

16GW629 Battle of Fromelles: men of the 53rd Battalion in their front line minutes before going over the top and across No Man's Land to attack the German lines.

16GW628 Part of the German front line at Fromelles after the attack. This photograph was taken on the morning of 20 July after the Germans had retaken this position. The Germans have covered the bodies of those who fell in the fighting with coats or blankets.

16GW634 Battle of Fromelles – Germans reoccupying their second line following the withdrawal by the Australians, 20 July. Evidence of attempts to consolidate the position by the Australians can be seen, where deepening of the trenches has taken place and sandbags have been repositioned. Lying about in the mud and water are the bodies of Australian soldiers killed in the fighting.

Bei Fromelles gef. Engl. 20.7.16

16GW1504 These photographs of Australian dead were taken after the Germans had retaken their trenches.

16GW1501, 16GW1502, 16GW1505 Australian dead gathered for burial at Fromelles.

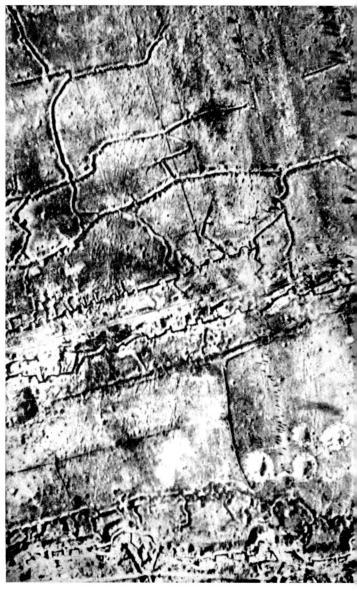

16GW630 Photograph taken across No Man's Land towards the German trenches, which were receiving a pounding prior to the attack by men of the 5th Australian Division in ten minutes time. The foliage is the remains of an old orchard hedge in No Man's Land.

16GW631 Aerial photograph taken at about 6 pm, on 19 July, during the Battle of Fromelles. Men of 14 Brigade, attacking between 8 and 15 Brigades, can be seen as dots (with shadows, towards bottom right) advancing over German-held ground at an early stage of the attack.

16GW644 The Chalk Pit, near Pozières, with a major track leading to the front line running past it – 28 August 1916.

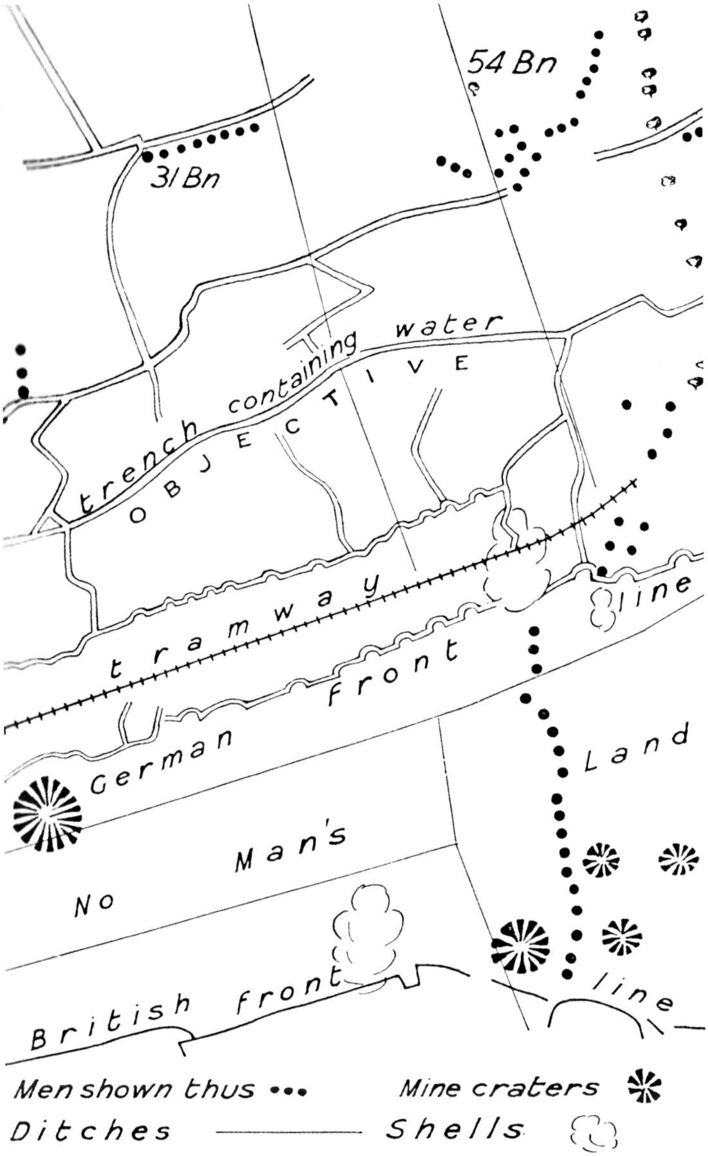
54 Bn
31 Bn
trench containing water
OBJECTIVE
tramway
German front line
No Man's Land
British front line
Men shown thus
Mine craters
Ditches
Shells

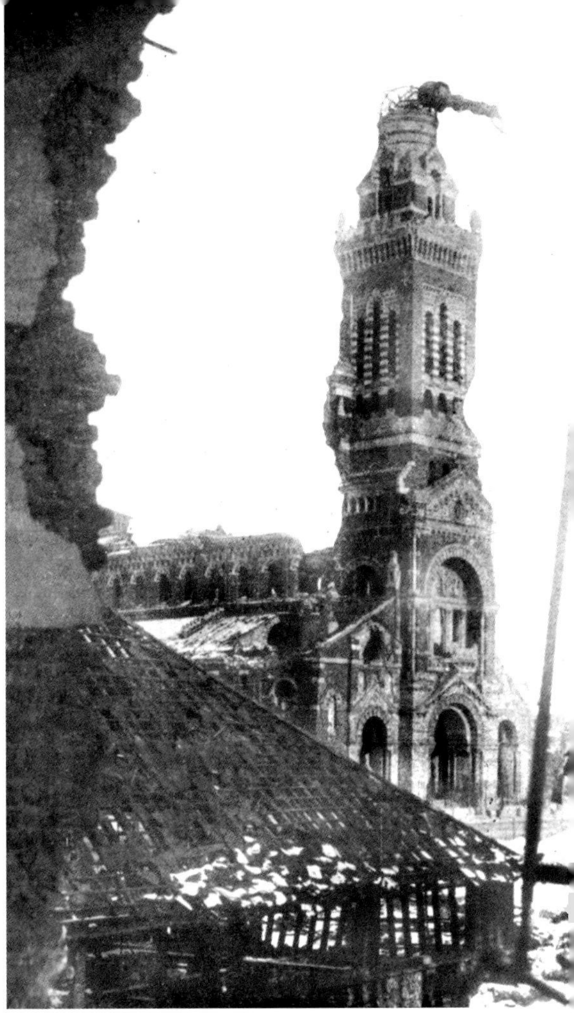

16GW642 Basilica of Notre-Dame de Brebières at Albert, on the Somme, with its leaning Virgin and Child. Passed by innumerable columns of men marching to and from the front line.

16GW646 Activity in Sausage Valley on 28 August during the fighting around Pozières.

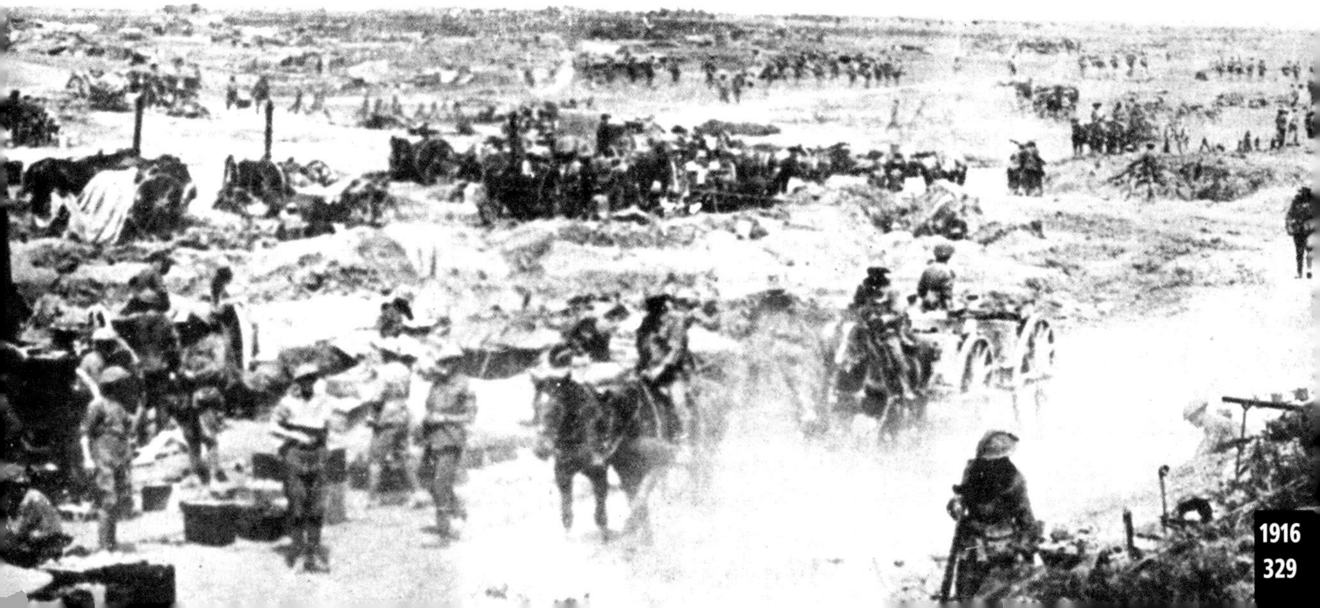

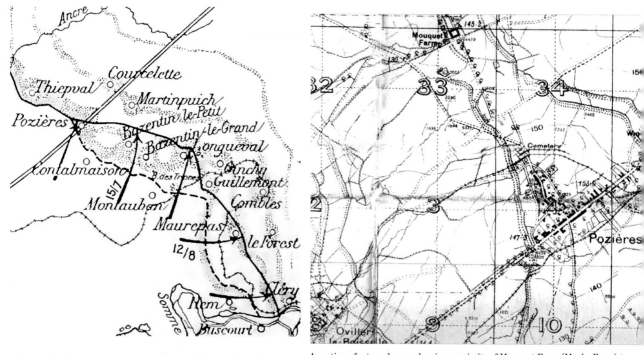

Franco-British advances on the north bank of the Somme to 15 July 1916.

A section of a trench map showing proximity of Mouquet Farm (Mucky Farm) to the village of Pozières.

16GW639 Pozières, 23 June, before the British barrage in preparation to the attack of 1 July 1916. The German defences consisted of three lines: K Trench; OG1 and OG2 (see key diagram opposite).

16GW652 Pozières before the Somme battle. A barn in the village during its occupation by the Germans.

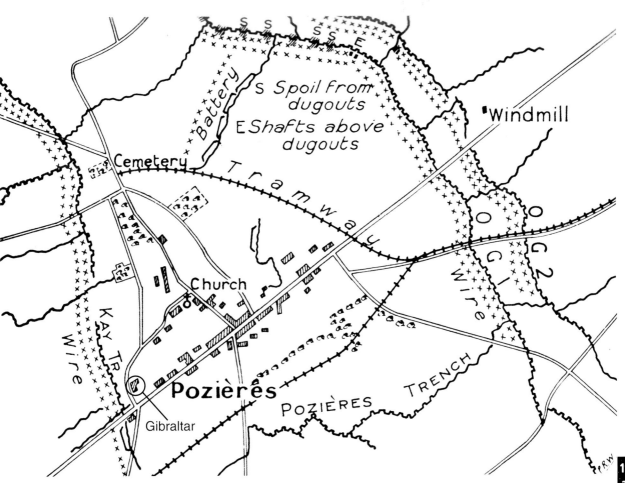

16GW653 An Australian trench mortar about to be fired from the Chalk Pit, 2 August.

16GW661 The pond at Pozières before the war. The pond was situated on the southern side of the main road running through the village.

16GW655, 16GW656 The main street through Pozières before the war. The view is from the corner near the church, looking towards The Windmill and Bapaume.

16GW654 What was left of the main street through Pozières. The view is from Centre Way, looking towards the Windmill. The bombardment by the British had been heavy, but the fire subsequently laid down by the German artillery was considered by many to be the heaviest and most protracted experienced by men of the AIF during the war.

16GW659a, The church at Pozières before the war. 16GW658 The church during the German occupation. 16GW659 Interior of the church 1 September 1915.

16GW669 Men of the 2nd Australian Division coming out of the line after their first tour at Pozières, 10 August. Here men of 6 Brigade are passing an audience consisting of men of 2 Brigade near Warloy-Baillon.

16GW657 Ruins of the Church at Pozières, 28 August 1916.

16GW664 A section of the Old German line ('OG 1'): entrances can be seen leading to the German deep dugouts. Australian attacks of 29 July and 4 August came from left to right. When these positions had been taken, further attacks were made towards Mouquet Farm (top of the picture).

16GW663 Remains of the wire in front of the lines. Photograph taken on 28 August 1916 from Centre Way and shows the old iron stakes of the entanglements in front of OG1.

16GW662 A neat and orderly German communication trench leading to Pozières in April 1916, before the fierce fighting turned the ground into an even more featureless landscape.

16GW666 Casualty Corner, 1 August 1916. These are men belonging to 5 and 6 Brigades.

16GW668 The courtyard of Mouquet Farm before the war. The farm lay a mile north of Pozières and was the country residence of the owner of a local factory. T[he] Germans, in fortifying it, excavated dugouts under the main farm buildings and also under the back buildings.

16GW671 The cellars beneath the rubble of Mouquet Farm. These stairways led down to long galleries and dugouts, which ran deep under the farm courtyard. These underground quarters could hold approximately 200 men.

16GW667 The courtyard of Mouquet Farm, 11 October, 1916. The scene shows the devastation after Australian, Canadian and British assaults on the German fortified farm.

16GW707 Mouquet Farm, showing the German trench system that incorporated the farm in the defence position.
16GW708 Aerial photograph after continual shelling.

16GW715 Ruins of Mouquet Farm, October 1916.

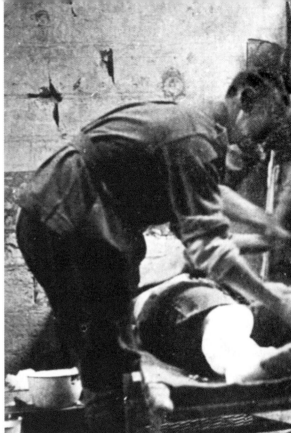

16GW673 A Field Dressing Station at Bécourt Château during the Battle of Pozières. It was used by the 2nd Australian Division.

16GW709 Wounded awaiting treatment.

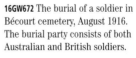

16GW672 The burial of a soldier in Bécourt cemetery, August 1916. The burial party consists of both Australian and British soldiers.

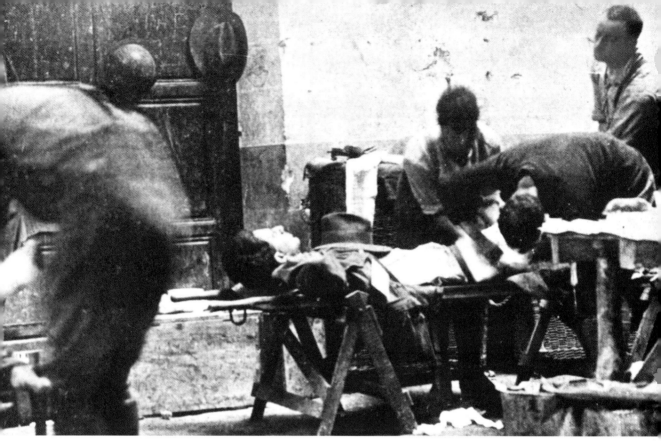

16GW716 The seemingly never ending job of filling sandbags.

16GW717 Mules employed in bringing up supplies.

16GW718 Australians with their mascot leaving the trenches.

16GW703 Road to Pozières, August 1916.

1916
345

16GW674 I Anzac Corps returning to the Somme in October 1916 to take part in a push towards Bapaume before winter closed in. The photograph shows men of 6 Infantry Brigade, 5th Australian Division, resting during the march down the mud choked road to Fricourt.

16GW678 The village of Gueudecourt as it was in March, 1915, when occupied by the Germans.

16GW675 A typical scene on the Somme front in November: Water carts and other mule drawn transport hauling through the mud at Montauban.

16GW676 The village of Flers looking eastwards from the church tower. This was early in the war, when the village was used by the Germans as a rest area.

16GW677 The village of Flers had been captured by the New Zealanders and British on 15 September. The village was now about a mile behind the front line and the cellars of the houses served as headquarters for a number of Australian units..

16GW679 The village of Gueudecourt in late 1916. Immediately in front of the village ran the southern part of the line assigned to I Anzac Corps during the major part of the winter. The village was incessantly shelled by the Germans and was a place to be avoided.

16GW682 Part of the front known as 'Fritz's Folly', a sunken road forming part of the German front line. This was attacked by the 1st and 3rd Battalions on the night of 4 November, 1916; an attack which failed, due in part to the muddy ground. The position was subsequently abandoned by the Germans and became a part of the Australian front line.

16GW680 The church and town pond at Flers, early in the war. The church was then being used by the Germans as a hospital.

16GW683 The Australian Support Line: Cheese Road was a sunken road in front of Flers. Shortly before this photograph was taken Brigadier General Glasfurd, commanding 12 Infantry Brigade, was mortally wounded by a German shell. He endured an agonizing ten hour stretcher journey before reaching an Advanced Dressing Station, but died that night.

16GW681 Part of the Support Line seen here during the Somme winter. Note the sandbags built across the Main Bapaume road at Le Sars. The Australians were here at the end of the winter.

16GW684 Biscuit Trench, a communication trench leading from near Cheese Road to the front line.

16GW686 Switch Trench, 23 November 1916, showing infantry of the the 1st Australian Division in 'rest'. With the battle formerly over, the usual procedure of rotating soldiers to the support and rear helped to alternate the dreadful conditions in the front line.

16GW719 Stretcher bearers and Padre, belonging to the 2nd Australian Division, bringing in a wounded man under a white flag.

16GW695 Part of the trench system near Flers improved by the I Anzac Corps.

16GW685 Gun Valley, west of Flers, where Australian field artillery was positioned for the winter.

16GW688 The Butte de Warlencourt, once an ancient mound covered in pine trees, had been incorporated into the German front line opposite the British at Le Sars. The mound was attacked by British and Australian infantry on the 5 November and again on the 14th. Both attacks failed.

16GW696 A working party, consisting of men from the 16th Battalion, cleaning Gird Trench, November.

16GW691 Australian wounded being conveyed on a tramway, constructed for transporting supplies, ammunition and wounded men.

16GW694 Men of an Australian infantry battalion moving up to the front from a reserve camp situated behind Delville Wood and which had Nissen huts as living quarters. These huts and the construction of duckboard walkways went a long way to alleviate some of the hardships being suffered during the winter of 1916-1917.

16GW701 France, December 1916. Men of the 5th Division enjoying a 'smoko' near Mametz, on the Somme. Some are wearing slouch hats, steel helmets, sheepskin jackets and woollen gloves, demonstrating both the variety of official battledress and how it was modified and augmented according to local conditions.

16GW692 Stretchering wounded through the Somme mud in December 1916. During this period it could take nine relays of stretcher bearers (thirty-six men) twelve hours to carry one wounded man from the front line to the dressing station situated three miles to the rear.

16GW690 Millencourt church, thirteen miles behind the front, was used at the end of the Battle of the Somme as a Main Dressing Station.

16GW697 Traffic in the snow near Méaulte. So long as the ground remained frozen it made movement easier.

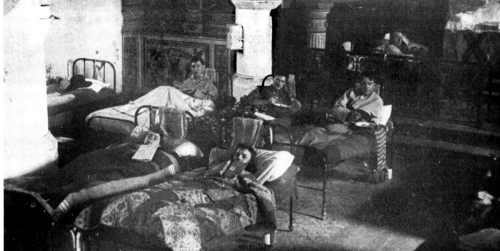

16GW687 Australian infantrymen drinking coffee at the Australian Comforts Fund stall, Longueval, December 1916. The men serving at the stall are Private A. Gunn and Private C. Neild. Both men were killed when a German booby trap mine exploded at Bapaume Town Hall during the night of 25 March 1917.

The Somme

With the British

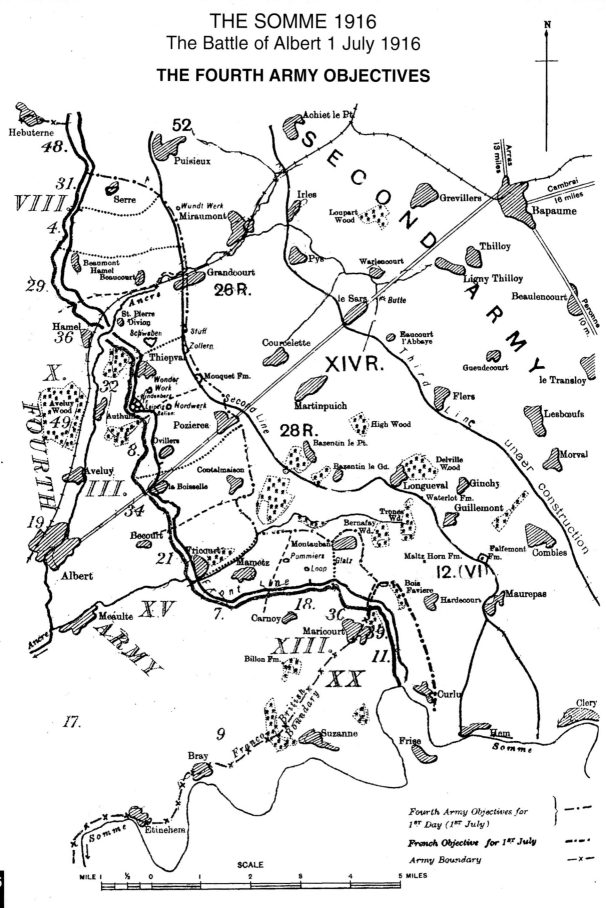

THE SOMME 1916
The Battle of Albert 1 July 1916
THE FOURTH ARMY OBJECTIVES

N

Fourth Army Objectives for 1ST Day (1ST July) — — —

French Objective for 1ST July — · — ·

Army Boundary — × —

SCALE

MILE 1   ½ 0   1   2   3   4   5 MILES

16GW723 General Joffre, Sir Douglas Haig and General Foch in 1916. Haig and the French generals agree on a plan for a joint summer offensive starting on or about 1 July.

In February 1916 Haig ordered General Rawlinson to take over planning the attack on the Somme. Rawlinson submitted his plan to Haig, suggesting an advance of between 1,000 and 3,000 yards on a 20,000 yard front running from the village of Serre in the north to Maricourt on the banks of the Somme River. Rawlinson's declared intention, was to 'kill as many Germans as possible with the least loss to ourselves'. He was asked to consider 'probable opportunities' for the use of cavalry to exploit any breakthrough. Haig, a cavalry man through and through, did not rate very highly the war's new weaponry. 'The machine gun is a much over rated weapon' was his judgement in 1915. He would change his mind following the Battle of the Somme.

16GW724 General Sir Henry Rawlinson and General Sir Douglas Haig at Fourth Army HQ, Querrieu, July 1916.

16GW731 Sir Douglas Haig, March 1916. The Guard of Honour is from the 23rd Battalion, London Regiment, 47th Division.

16GW728 Haig's confidence was high that cavalry would be employed to exploit the breakthrough that was bound to occur.

16GW729 Indian cavalry practise a cavalry charge behind the lines on the Somme front.

16GW727 Cavalry on the move behind the lines on the Somme front.

16GW732 British Transport Lines near Fricourt,1916. Transport of the 51st Highland Division.

16GW730 The Deccan Horse on the Carnoy-Mametz road,1916.

16GW733 Artillery camp by the roadside prior to the Somme offensive.

16GW734 British troops rehearsing the move across No Man's Land towards the German machine guns.

16GW735 Mules look on as traction engines haul heavy guns to artillery postions behind the British front.

16GW737 British Cyclists Company. Not a mode of transportation for a complete battalion, that would survive the five years of modern warfare.

16GW736 Teams of eight cart horses pulling 8-inch howitzers to artillery lines ready for the British Summer offensive.

16GW738 Bringing up supplies for the Great Push by lorries.

16GW739 A constant flow of supplies were needed to keep an army in the field – much more so during an offensive.

16GW740 Neat stacks of 18-pounder shells.

16GW746, 16GW744, 16GW743. Ammunition for the mighty 15-inch howitzer which could hurl a shell a distance of over five miles. Chalking 'cheeky' messages on some projectiles was good for the morale of the British gunners and for film viewers back home.

16GW741 18-pounder shells and a British Tommy pretending (surely) to sleep on the munitions.

16GW742 Shells for the British 15-inch howitzer. There were too few of this type of gun for the operations that began on 1 July.

16GW749 Shells delivered and awaiting feeding into this camouflaged 15-inch howitzer.

16GW745,16GW748,16GW747. Bombs for the 2-inch trench mortar; nicknamed the 'Toffee Apple' and 'Plum Pudding'.

16GW750, 16GW751. Work parties preparing positions on the Somme for the forthcoming Big Push, planned for late June 1916.

16GW753,16GW754. The 1/14th (County of London) Battalion, London Scottish, marching up for the diversionary attack on the village of Gommecourt by the 56th (London) Division.

16GW756, 16GW755. A battalion of the East Yorkshire Regiment marching to take its position on the Somme front.

16GW758, 16GW757. The Royal Welsh Fusiliers

16GW752 Men of the Worcestershire Regiment on the Acheux road leading to the trenches.

16GW759, 16GW760.
A battalion of the Hampshire Regiment, with stretcher bearers bringing up the rear with their cumbersome loads. Note one of them clowning as he takes a bow for the camera; they were all in the best of spirits.

16GW761 Men of the 1st Battalion, Wiltshire Regiment, on the Acheux road leading to the trenches. Some of them have barbed wire cutters on their rifles.

16GW762 A Lewis gun section of the 10th Battalion, East Yorkshire Regiment, near Doullens, July 1916.

16GW763 A wiring party going to the front line trenches after collecting stores. A water and air pump at this Royal Engineers dump gives evidence of possible mining operations being carried out under the German trenches.

1916
372

16GW764, 16GW765. The shelled Basilica of Notre-Dame de Brebières in Albert, three miles behind the British front. The statue of Mary and the infant Jesus hanging from the tower gave rise to the superstition that whichever side in the conflict caused it to topple to the ground would lose the war. British soldiers marching to and from the front became very familiar with the leaning 'Virgin of Albert'.

16GW766, 16GW767. Men of a battalion of the Manchester Regiment at Church Parade receiving assurance from the padre that the Almighty is most certainly on their side. This will lead to bitter disillusion for many when the Germans, wearing the slogan *Gott Mit Uns* (God With Us) on their army belts, inflict heavy casualties and British attacks generally meet with little success.

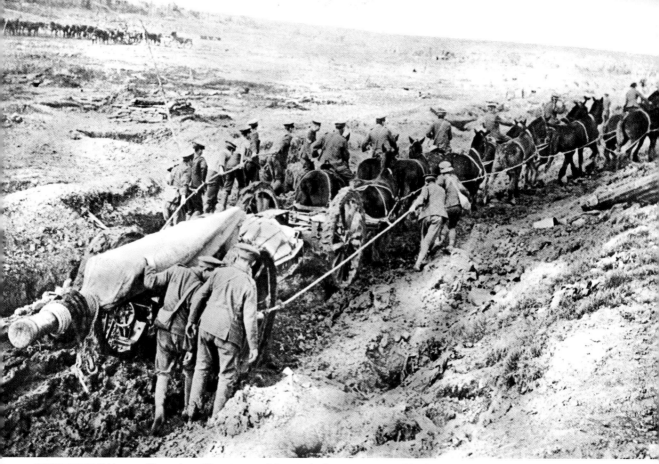

16GW770,16GW770. Taking up a 60-pounder artillery piece, emplying a twelve-horse team, to a position from which to bombard the German lines prior to the full scale British Infantry attack scheduled for the end of June. Manhandling the weapon through the ruts and in the soggy ground conditions.

16GW779,16GW780,16GW781,16GW782 British 4.7-inch gun firing on the German held village of Mametz, June 1916, days before the Great Push: sighting and laying the weapon; about to be fired by a lanyard; firing and recoil; clearing the shell case and relaying the weapon.

16GW783 Crew of a 9.2-inch howitzer engaged in a barrage against Geman positions.

16GW784 Moving an 8-inch howitzer to a new position, summer 1916

16GW785 The BL 8-inch howitzer Mark I, a British improvization developed to provide heavy artillery. It used shortened and bored-out barrels from various redundant naval 6-inch guns. It remained in use on the Western Front throughout the war.

16GW793, 16GW795, 16GW796, 16GW798, 16GW797, 16GW794,

Loading and firing a 15-inch howitzer. The weight of the shells required the use of a chain hoist system to lift the them. It could throw a 1,400 lb heavy shell six miles and some considered it hardly worth all the labour and time it took to move and emplace these very heavy guns. However, one round a minute could be achieved by an efficient and well trained gun crew.

Newspaper correspondent, Philip Gibbs wrote: *'The guns slammed sharply with hard metalic knocks. The glib phrase "the thunder of guns" hardly describes accurately the series of enormous strikes upon invisible anvils it truely resembled.'*

16GW786 Carnoy Valley, July 1916. The 18-pounder was first produced in 1904. In August 1914 the British Army had 1,226 of them. By the end of the war the army had upward of nine and a half thousand in service.

16GW788 Empty shell cases – a graphic image indicating the volume of explosives being hurled at the German positions prior to the Great Push

16GW787 An 18-pounder in action near Authuille.

16GW789 A battery of Royal Artillery howitzers bombarding the German trenches before the opening of the Battle of the Somme.

16GW790, 16GW792. After a week long barrage, when dawn came on 1 July 1916 bursting artillery shells reached a cresendo. All the British infantry would have to do was to walk over and take the battered German trenches.

16GW791 Major General Sir Beauvoir de Lisle addresses a battalion of the 29th Division on the eve of the Somme battle.

16GW799 Awaiting an underground mine to explode under the German positions on Hawthorn Ridge which was to signal the attack along a twenty-five mile front by eighteen British and French infantry divisions.

The largest assault in the history of warfare, to date, began on Saturday morning 1 July 1916. The Franco-British attack had been fully expected to succeed and the overwhelming of the German defences was supposed to be occuring along a twenty-five mile front. It was not happening, apart from in the south, where the British-held line butted up to the French. The British 30th Division, which comprised mainly Manchester and Liverpool Pals battalions, swept through – as envisaged by the planning generals – and captured the German-held village of Montauban. Also there was success in capturing the village of Mametz by the 7th Division and then Fricourt the following day. The French had a successful first day, gaining nearly all their objectives. Elsewhere along the front it was a disaster. North of the Albert-Bapaume road the British made little progress against the German defences, apart from a small gain at the Leipzig Redoubt, to the south west of Thiepval. They had failed and been turned back in front of the German fortified villages of Gommecourt, Serre, Beaumont Hamel, Thiepval and La Boisselle. Casualties were a staggering 57,000, the highest battlefield casualty figure ever suffered by the British Army. The futile struggle to push German forces holding high ground positions off French territory placed about the River Somme would go on until November.

16GW800 Men of 86 Brigade wait for the whistles to blow, signalling the attack.

16GW1089, 16GW1090, 16GW1091. The Sunken Road in No Man's Land, the 1st Battalion, Lancashire Fusiliers waiting for the signal to begin their attack on Beaumont Hamel. As they left this cover at 7.30 am, 1 July, they came under fire from Beaumont Hamel and Hawthorn Ridge. Eighteen officers and 465 men were lost during the day's fighting. The road became known as Hunter's Lane.

16GW1100, 16GW1104, 16GW1106
Infantry resting in support
trenches before the attack.

16GW1101 Lancashire Fusiliers
fixing bayonets, ready to climb
from their trench and walk
towards the German barbed wire
at zero hour.

16GW1105 Four Royal Engineers officers in a support trench on 1 July 1916, with the attack well under way.

16GW1092 Ten minutes before zero the Hawthorn Mine was blown, giving the Germans, who had rushed to occupy the crater caused by the explosion, sufficient time to prepare to meet the attacking British infantry. At 7.30am men of the 29th Division moved forward and walked into a hail of death.

16GW1093 Men of the Wiltshire Regiment passing through their own wire as they are launched against the fortified village of Thiepval. The German strongpoint would eventually fall in late September.

16GW1093 The Tyneside Irish (24th, 25th, 26th and 27th Battalions Northumberland Fusiliers) attacking towards La Boisselle. *The mines went off and a few minutes later 103 Brigade began coming over the hill in beautifully regular lines, dressing and intervals maintained as well as on a ceremonial parade. Everyone felt proud of that lot of Tynesiders.*
History of the 18th Battalion (Pioneers) Northumberland Fusiliers.

The brigade suffered heavy casualties even before its battalions reached the British front-line. The brigade's losses on 1 July were so severe that a few days later it was transferred to the 37th Division to recover and be brought back up to strength.

16GW1096 Tyneside Irish: as the leading wave moves off, the second wave can be seen about to stand up and follow.

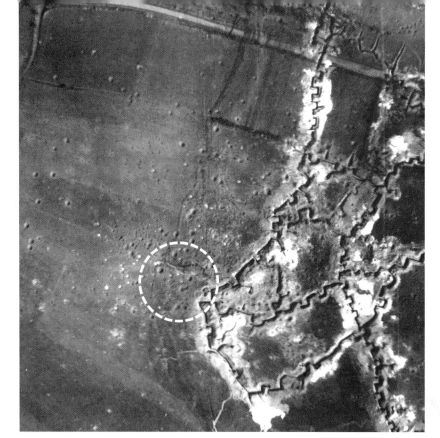

16GW1108 NCOs and men of a company of the Public Schools Battalion 16th Middlesex Regiment, at a position behind the lines White City prior to the 1 July attack on German positions on Hawthorn and Redan ridges.

16GW1107 Ten minutes after the British mine was exploded under the German trenches on Hawthorn Ridge the infantry attacked. Ten minutes was sufficient time for German reserves to occupy the lip of the mine crater and pour fire into the attackers. Here we see survivors of C and D Companies, 16th (Public Schools) Battalion, The Middlesex Regiment, running back across No Man's Land after their failed attempt to seize the Hawthorne Crater lip.

16GW1247 Men of the Middlesex Regiment, crawling in No Man's Land on their way back to the British lines.

16GW1097, 16GW1098. Y Sap Crater, one of two mines blown in this sector on 1 July under the German positions at La Boisselle. The attack was not successful, despite the mines blown and losses sustained, particularly by the Tyneside Scottish. Other battalions of the 34th Division lost heavily. In the photographs the ground is littered with dead and wounded men from Tyneside.

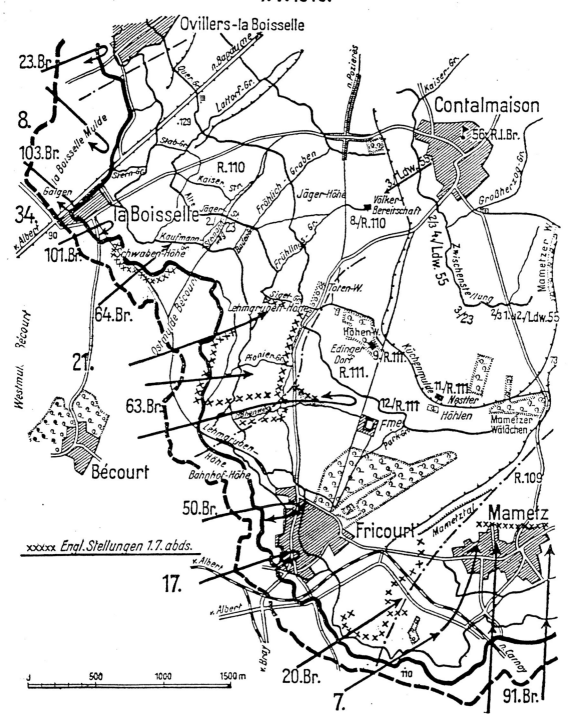

La Boisselle - Fricourt
1. 7. 1916.

A German map depicting the fighting in the La Boisselle–Fricourt area during the opening assault here on the first day of the Battle of the Somme

16GW1102 Men of the 7th Division can be seen against the white, chalky soil approaching the German trenches in front of Mametz.

16GW1099 Trenches captured by the 11th Battalion, Cheshire Regiment, at Ovillers-la-Boisselle, on the Somme, July 1916. A sentry keeps watch while others sleep.

16GW1103 Trophies galore to be found in these captured German trenches at Fricourt. Among the items are rifles, boots, canteens and a trench torch. Such snaps are rare as privately owned cameras were forbidden. Official photographers were supplying all images for press releases. Compare the well-posed picture above with the ilicit snap. Cameras were forbidden and was strictly enforced. A British official photographer only appeared in 1916.

16GW1114 Germans killed in the preliminary shelling.

16GW1117 A British soldier covers the face of a German in a captured trench.

16GW1119 Built to last, these steps lead to underground shelters at the northern corner of Bernafay Wood, captured on 3 July 1916.

16GW1118, 16GW1120. This entrance to a deep German dugout revealed the level of protection enjoyed by the invaders, who had constructed their shelters for a long stay on the ground they had captured. British officers enjoy the comforts of home left by the Germans.

16GW1121 Captured ground at La Boisselle; although the trenches have been shelled almost flat, entrances to the deep dugouts are still evident.

16GW1123 Filling sandbags to repair and reconfigure recently captured trenches. The German trenches had to be reversed

16GW1122 Captured trench littered with German dead.

16GW1110 A first of July casualty, a wounded German prisoner at La Boisselle.

16GW1126 Curious onlookers watch as prisoners taken in the later Somme fighting pass along the roadway for imprisonment and, in the case of the wounded, medical care. No doubt some choice comments and witticisms were being called out by the Tommies.

16GW1124 Prisoners under escort, one wounded, from the Somme fighting.

16GW1125 British Walking wounded (with a German medical orderly), casualties from the fighting at Bernafay Wood, Montauban, July 1916.

16GW1129, 16GW1130, 16GW1128. Captured Germans being collected for marching across what was once No Man's Land to the prisoner of war cages. Walking wounded and stretcher cases bring up the rear.

16GW1127 A prisoner of war barbed wire compound, with a smattering of Germans captured in the first day of the Somme fighting. It had been fully anticipated by the planners of the attack that these cages would be packed with prisoners on the first day of the Big Push.

16GW1113 A company sergeant major takes the roll call of these survivors of the attack by the Lancashire Fusiliers.

16GW1112 Germans have lined up the bodies of these British soldiers for burial. Note that their boots, prized booty, have been removed.

16GW1111 A British wounded man of the 29th Division being carried the quick way through the British trench system – on the back of a comrade.

16GW1115, 16GW1116 All along the Somme front the British trenches were choked with wounded as the German counter barrage and machine gun fire took its toll on the attackers.

16GW1131 The Advanced Dressing Station at Minden Post, 7th Division, where lightly wounded men of 91 Brigade are being cared for.

16GW1134, 16GW1135, 16GW1136. The soldier has been shot clean through his left arm. He has also been injured in his shoulder.

16GW1137, 16GW1138. The Advanced Dressing Station at Minden Post.

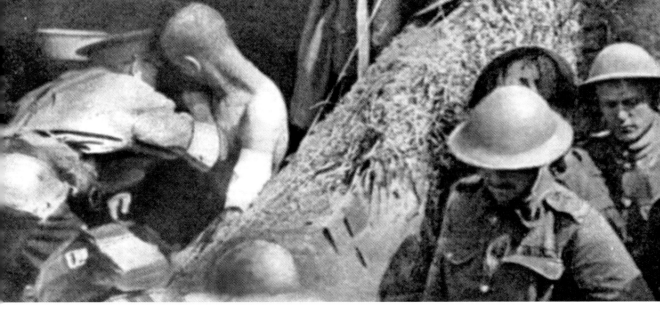

16GW1139, 16GW1140. After the Walking Wounded Collecting Stations and Advanced Dressing Stations, (or Collecting Posts), wounded men were transported either to an Advanced Operative Centre or a Main Dressing Station. After the disastrous attacks on 1 July all medical facilities were stretched beyond all estimates.

16GW1147 Some of the walking wounded.

Casualty Clearing Stations had capacity for only 9,500 cases, In the event, the number of British wounded, amounted to 38,230. With medical facilities overwhelmed, many casualties were left in the open untended and it was three days before the Fourth Army medical services had treated all the wounded. The number killed on that first day amounted to 19,240,

16GW1148 One of the hospital barges operating on French canals.

16GW1149 Operations were carried out at the Advanced Operative Centre in Casualty Clearing Stations.

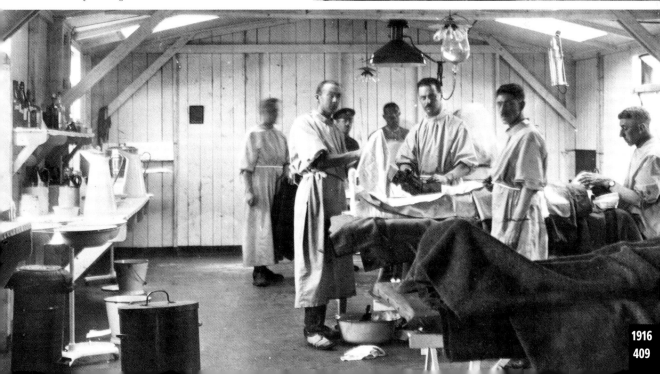

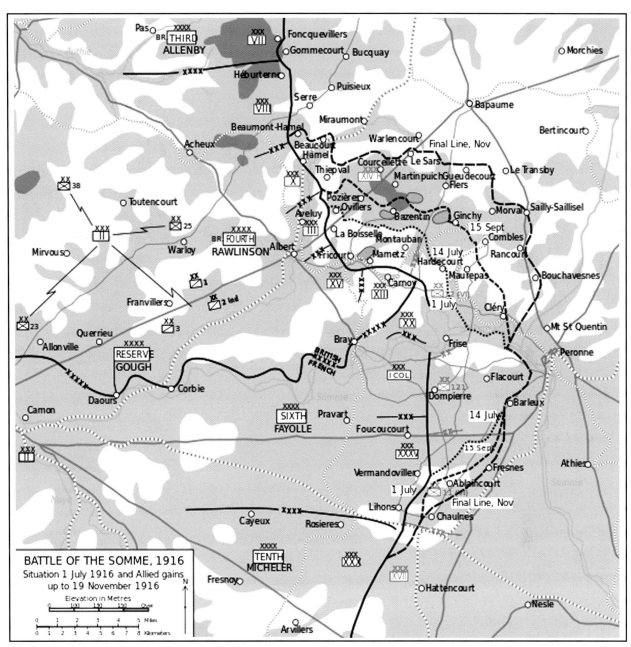

BATTLE OF THE SOMME, 1916
Situation 1 July 1916 and Allied gains
up to 19 November 1916

Elevation in Metres

16GW1153 Soldiers' large packs, not carried by the attacking infantry, have to be sorted through. They often contained the soldier's great coat or blanket, along with personal effects.

Douglas Haig wrote in his diary for the first of July:

North of the Ancre, VIII Corps said they began well, but as the day progressed, their troops were forced back into the German front line, except two battalions which occupied Serre village, and were, it is said, cut off. I am inclined to believe from further reports that few of VIII Corps left their trenches.

The men in the divisions of VIII Corps had left their trenches and its casualties amounted to over 14,000 dead and wounded.

1916
412

16GW1145 Understandably, those who lost their menfolk needed to believe that they had received a decent burial and had died painlessly. This a press release picture with an official caption: *Words are read over the graves of two Tommies killed in the fighting near Ovillers, July 1916.*

16GW1144 The dead are collected and searched for identification before being buried. German soldiers and British prisoners are working together to get the job done.

16GW1143 A mass grave being filled in. This is a burial by German troops and the British carried the task out in the same way. Photographs like this were not for the public; rather, burials were usually shown as in single graves, with mourners gathered round.

16GW1141 British dead at a roadside behind the lines on the Somme. Further along two dead horses and a broken cart indicate shelling; blast and shrapnel may have taken their lives.

16GW1142 Death cheated on this occasion: this Tommy proudly displays his damaged helmet where shrapnel ripped through and gave him a scalp wound.

16GW1150 British soldiers clearing a captured village where fighting and shelling has left devastation.

16GW1151 British rifles collected and stacked for the armourers to sort through and either make repairs or scrap them.

16GW1152 British Lee Enfield rifles, their former owners either wounded or dead, being collected from the battlefield. Note that many have bayonets fitted, indicating that they they were dropped during an attack.

16GW1155 Men of the Sherwood Foresters wearing *pickelhaube* helmets and showing off Luger pistols, bayonets and a switchboard telephone apparatus, captured from the Germans.

16GW1156 Artillery men examine a captured German 77mm Field Gun M96nA. This was the principal field gun built by Krupp and was used throughout the war.

16GW1157 The weapon that caused so much damage among the ranks of attacking British infantrymen – the German 08 Maxim machine gun.

16GW1158 A pioneer battalion works to repair and improve a road. In the distance a column of marching men.

16GW1159, 16GW1160. Working party of a Highland regiment clearing and repairing a road on the Somme to keep the advance moving along as gains are exploited.

16GW1161 Fresh water, a vital commodity for an army in the field.

16GW1163 Cans – the same as those used for petrol except with a green rather than a red cap – were used to carry precious water supplies to the front line.
16GW1162 An underground pipe brings water to a stand positioned by a narrow gauge rail line.

16GW1164 Former German trench shelters now in use by British Tommies.

16GW1167 A company of the 1st Battalion, Royal Warwickshire Regiment. The battalion was in reserve near Beaumont Hamel on 1 July 1916.

16GW1165 The BL 8-inch howitzer Mark I.

16GW1166 Stacks of shells to support and sustain the constant attacks by the British Fourth Army on the Somme.

16GW1168 On the Sunken Road between La Boisselle and Contalmaison, men of a Highland battalion wait for orders to deploy and follow a creeping barage towards the German lines.

16GW1169 Infantry waiting their turn to advance during the Battle of Morval, late September 1916.

16GW1170, 16GW1171 Support troops consolidating captured German trenches.

16GW1172, 16GW1173 Captured positions at Guillemont, with corpses choking the trenches.

16GW1174, 16GW1177 Main street, Guillemont, the village no longer recognizable. An Advanced Dressing Station at Guillemont.

16GW1178 German prisoners being used to carry wounded on stretchers away from the fighting. Note that one prisoner is carrying a rifle slung over his shoulder

16GW1179 Stretcher bearers bringing in a wounded comrade pass a dead horse with a severed neck. A large piece of shrapnel from a shell must have done this damage.

16GW1180 An enormous explosion from the direction of the fighting arrests the attention of the chaplain, medical orderlies and wounded at this Advanced Dressing Station.

16GW1181 Motor ambulances at this Main Dressing Station ready to take wounded to a Casualty Clearing Station.

16GW1182, 16GW1184, 16GW11843, 16GW1185. These images, taken by an official British Army photographer, capture in vivid scenes a twentieth century battlefield: the terrible results caused by shelling and machine guns – torn ground and torn men. These bloated, fly-covered human remains had to be searched for identification and moved for burial. Enthusiastic notions of glory in military prowess and feats of acclaimed heroism faded for thousands of soldiers on both sides as men became disillusioned, following the horrific battles of Verdun and the Somme in 1916. Battles of the following year would serve to underline the foolishness of nations seeking dominence, then settling the resulting disputes by fighting.

16GW1188 A British corporal surveys the devastation caused by a shell exploding on a German trench in the fighting near Guillemont. The British had improved the effectiveness of their artillery-fire, partly through experience and partly of developing techniques, such as improved collaboration with aircraft. Note that the NCO seems to have acquired a German pistol and is wearing a leather belt and holster. Capture of the village of Guillemont was the culmination of British attacks which had begun on 22/23 July. The British Fourth Army took the village in early September. The next village to capture was Ginchy, north-east of Guillemont and less than a mile away.

16GW1187 German prisoners being marched to the rear. Note the tank: this new weapon was devised by the British to roll across and overcome barbed wire defences and allow the infantry assaults to bring about that sought after breakthrough.

16GW1186 Captured Germans are pass a sign indicating that it is a Guards Division dump.

16GW1196 A slightly injured soldier making his way back through the trenches for his wound to be attended at an Advanced Dressing Station in Mametz Wood.

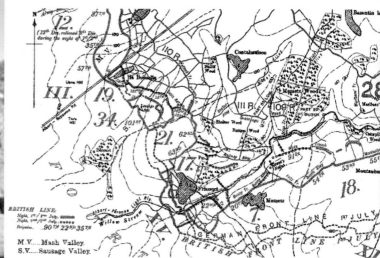

16GW1189 Mametz Wood: although the fortified village of Mametz was taken on the opening day of the Somme, fighting to drive the Germans out of Mametz Wood would last for a further ten days.

16GW1197 The main street in Mametz; the village was captured on the first day of the Battle of the Somme.

16GW1193 A German observation post built in a tree near the southern edge of Mametz Wood.

16GW1195 An abandoned German gun at Mametz.

16GW1190 Mametz Wood: A Royal Field Artillery battery moves to a new position. An exchange of wit seems to be in progress – likely with reference to the camera.

16GW1192, 16GW1191. German ammunition wagons destroyed by artillery fire, close to Mametz Wood.

16GW1199 A German artillery piece after a direct hit,

16GW1198 A German gun abandoned in Mametz Wood. The breech mechanism has been removed

16GW1204 A captured German gun in position in Mametz Wood.

16GW1207 Gordon Highlanders out of the line for a rest, Mametz Wood.

16GW1205 The 15th Battalion, Hampshire Regiment, resting before going into the trenches. Southern Road, Mametz Wood, 17 July 1916. Note the ambulances on the road by the wood.

16GW1200 Newly hollowed out shelters for the British reserves near Mametz.

16GW1206 Stretcher bearers, initially formed in peacetime units from the bandsmen in a battalion; however, casualties changed this arrangement.

16GW1265 Some men of the 5th Division who helped capture Morval, 25 September.

16GW1268 Tank D7 stuck in a shell hole; three of the crew, wearing their distinctive leather helmets, can be seen taking shelter with the infantry.

16GW1263 Delville Wood 1916. A hand-written note on the back of this photograph reads: *A few scattered members of my own battalion, 16th King's Royal Rifle Corps, after the first few weeks of the battle on the Somme. This wood was thick with trees previous to the 1916 onslaught.*

16GW1264 Delville Wood after its capture.

16GW1267 Cookhouse activity at Thiepval.

16GW1266 Stretcher bearers at Thiepval.

16GW1270 A shell damaged railway carriage makes a dry billet for these Tommies.

16GW1269 The railway station near Beaumont Hamel.

16GW1271 Cemetery at Beaumont Hamel. Writing on the back of photograph: *All that remained of the cemetery and village when the 51st Division on our right on November 13/16 took it. Square stone pile in the foreground is remainder of German monument to their 1914 fallen.*

The Somme

With the Canadians

16GW1211 Wearing of the kilt was popular among some men in the newly-raised Canadian Expeditionary Force. A Highland Regiment arrives in Valcartier Camp for training. Three of the original seventeen infantry battalions of what was designated The First Contingent CEF were kilted.

16GW1209 Major General Arthur Currie, commander of the 1st Canadian Division on the Somme.

16GW1215 Inspection of men of the 38th Battalion before going overseas in 1915.

The General Service Badge of the Canadian Expeditionary Force

16GW1218 The RMS *Andania*, built for Cunard's London-Canada run, arriving in England.

16GW1217 Two battalions of the CEF, the 14th and 16th, leaving Quebec aboard the *Andania* in 1914.

16GW1210 Volunteers at the training camp at Valcartier, northwest of Quebec City. By September 1914, sixteen battalions had been created, numbered sequentially from the 1st to the 16th. The 5th, 6th, 7th, 8th, 9th, 10th and 11th battalions all came from Western Canada. Each battalion had an established strength of about 1,000 officers and men.

Manitoba Free Press.

VOL. 41.   WEATHER FORECAST. Weather unchanged.   Sun rises, 6.33 a.m.; sets, 5.84 p.m. Moon rises, 7.14 p.m.; sets, 11.46 a.m.   WINNIPEG, THURSDAY, OCTOBER 8, 1914.   EIGHTEEN PAGES.   NO. 82.

CANADIAN TROOPS REACH ENGLAND

French Army Regains Ground in Roye District

London Official Statement Reports Hard Fighting at Lens —Throughout Battle-line Conditions Generally Are Considered Satisfactory—French Soldiers Are Fighting With Greatest Dash and Bravery—German Cavalry Held In Check North of Lille.

London, October 7.—The official press bureau at 8 o'clock this evening issued the following statement:—

—North of the Oise and at Lens there is hard fighting. Elsewhere a slight advance or retreat varies. Throughout the line the reports are generally satisfactory.

"The French army is fighting with the greatest dash and

Despatches received early this morning announce the arrival in England of the first Canadian contingent of 33,000 men. The gigantic operation of transporting this large force across the Atlantic, requiring no less than thirty-three transports for its accommodation, has thus been safely accomplished. The transports were convoyed from Quebec by eleven warships, and it was understood that these would be joined by reinforcements in mid-Atlantic. The troops will proceed immediately to an inland destination at one of the numerous training camps, there to complete the preparations necessary for their eventual position as part of the enormous array pitted against the Germans.

BELGIAN CAPITAL MOVED TO OSTEND

Several Ministers With Personal Staffs Transferred at Noon Yesterday—Number of Refugees Flee to Holland from Antwerp—Fighting of Violent Character Taking Place Between Audenaide and Leupeghem Where Germans Are Repulsed After Belgians Received Reinforcements.

Amsterdam, October 7.—The Nieuwe Van Den Dag says that the t—

Germans Continue Offer Tenacious Resistance

Bring Up Reinforcements from Konigsberg to Oppose Advance of Russian Army—Beyond Vistula Advance Guard Battles Have Occurred in Region of Opatow and Sandomir—Petrograd Denies Growth of Anti-Russian Feeling In Persia.

Petrograd, October 7.—The Russian general staff today issued the following statement:—

"On the East Prussian frontier the Germans, having brought up reinforcements from Konigsberg, continue to offer tenacious resistance upon the battle front of Vladislavoff and Rutchka, profiting by the defiles, lakes and marshes in the region of Tchernoganja.

In August 1916, the Canadian Corps moved from Flanders to the Somme, where it took over a section of the line west of the village of Courcelette.

In the major offensive which began at dawn on 15 September 1916, the 2nd Division and a brigade of the 3rd Division of the Corps, was on the extreme left of the attack, a sector west of the village of Courcelette. They were aided by a new weapon of war – the tank. The attack was successful. Through September and October the three Canadian divisions attacked a series of German entrenchments. The final Canadian objective was Regina Trench, which repeatedly defied capture, and when the first three divisions were relieved in the middle of October, Regina Trench was a deal closer, but still in enemy hands. Finally, on 11 November 1916, the recently arrived 4th Division captured Regina Trench. In the final attack, the Canadians advanced to Desire Trench and there the Battle of the Somme staggered to a halt in the mud and cold of another winter.

16GW1222 A new revolutionary weapon of war designed to smash through the German defences and spearhead a breakthrough for the infantry – the tank. Its debut would coincide with that of the Canadian Corps acting in the capacity of a united fighting formation.

16GW1219 Lieutenant General The Hon Sir Julian Hedworth George Byng, commanding the Canadian Corps.

16GW1221 The Canadian allotment of the new weapon for the Battle of Flers-Courcelette was six tanks, to be used as part of the initial assault. Note the soldiers viewing the iron monster with curiosity, no doubt wondering what sort of a show it would be putting up against the Germans.

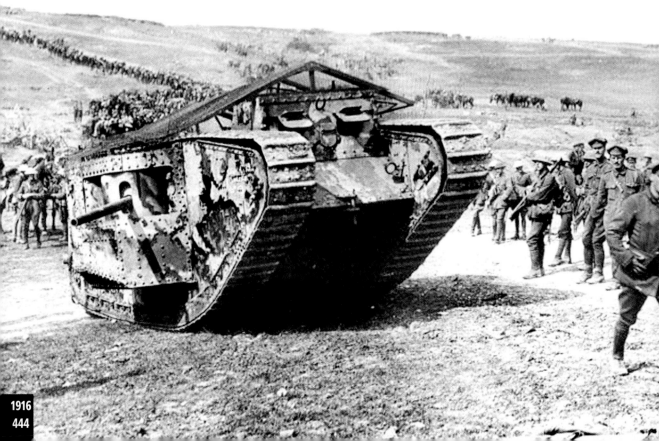

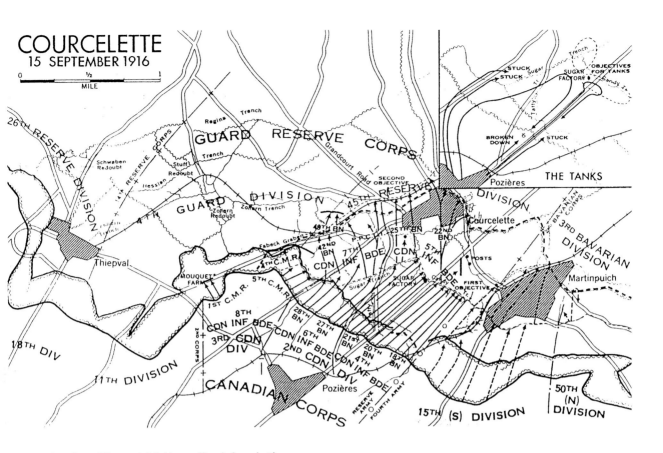

COURCELETTE
15 SEPTEMBER 1916

0 ½ 1
MILE

16GW1208 Canadian soldiers are briefed by an officer before a battle.

16GW1227 The new weapon, the tank, with Canadian infantry practise working together. At least it would provide some cover from German machine gun bullets.

16GW1225 Canadians testing a Vickers machine gun is the original caption, but it is more likely a posed picture for the camera.

16GW1250 A Canadian Scottish battalion, led by its drums, on parade. They would soon find themselves in the nightmare that was the front line in later 1916 on the Somme.

16GW1241 Courcelette in July 1916, when occupied by Germans.

16GW1237 Canadian artillerymen swabbing out the breech of a 9.2-inch howitzer.

16GW1226 Canadians attack the village of Courcelette, 15 September 1916; 'Fix bayonets!'
16GW1242 'Over the top – charge!' A staged photograph taken behind the lines.
16GW1243 Canadians consolidating the ground captured – around them are their comrades who were killed in the attack.

16GW1245 The Sugar Refinery, close to the main Albert-Bapaume road, just to the west of Courcelette, was used by the Germans as a strong point.

16GW1246 One of the German defenders of the positions around Courcelette, killed in the fighting.

16GW1244 The Sunken Lane, on the east side of Courcelette.

16GW1248, 16GW1249 The trenches and ground in the immediate area around Courcelette was littered with the fallen of both sides

16GW1254, 16GW1258, 16GW1256, 16GW1257. The wrecked village of Courcelette, now peopled by the brutally killed.

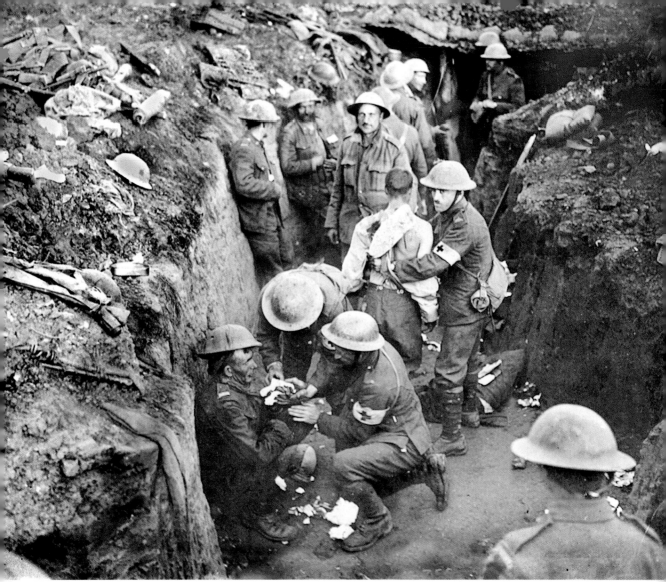

16GW1251,16GW1252, 16GW1253. First aid being given to the wounded in this trench in Courcelette after the fighting has moved on. The next step in caring for the wounded and injured is at a Main Dressing Station. Horse drawn ambulances here wait to take stretcher cases back to a Casualty Clearing Station. Labels attached to each man indicates the nature of his wound and treatment thus far.

16GW1255 A light railway being used to transport a Vickers machine gun and ammunition; a wounded soldier is being brought back on the trolley.

16GW1239,16GW1230. German prisoners taken during the fighting at Courcelette. Officers lead the march to the prison stockade. Note the Canadian Mounted Policeman at the front of the column.

16GW1236,16GW1260. Roads obliterated in the fighting had to be rebuilt to supply the next battles; Canadian Scots on fatigues along the Albert-Bapaume Road.

16GW1262 Canadians wheeling a wounded comrade along a muddy track that passed for a road.

16GW1235 Canadians moving to the rear after fighting around Courcelette.

16GW1232 Canadian victors, some wearing trophies taken at the Battle of Courcelette.

16GW1235 Canadian troops leaving the front line trenches while relief units move in. Autumn is turning and muddy conditions worsen, threatening another cold winter and with no sign of victory for the allies.

16GW1229, 16GW1228
Early Christmas messages of 'goodwill' for the Germans (not that they would be able to read them) chalked on guns and shells by the Canadians. The messages are for the camera man to record and for the people back home to enjoy.

16GW1194 'A Busting Time this Christmas 1916' chalked on a 5-inch shell.

The Somme

Winter

16GW1078 A working party, ankle deep in mud, near Bernafay Wood, November 1916.

16GW1085 The Royal Artillery moving 60-pounder guns by means of eight paired horse teams.

16GW1086 Repositioning an 8-inch howitzer in worsening weather conditions.

16GW1087 French and British soldiers sorting through equipment in a captured German trench.

The Battle of the Ancre Heights (1 October – 11 November 1916) was a continuation of the fighting on Thiepval Ridge in September, by the Reserve Army (renamed the Fifth Army on 30 October). British possession of the heights above the Ancre Valley would deprive the Germans of observation towards Albert to the south-west and give the British observation north over the Ancre valley to the German positions around Beaumont Hamel, Serre and Beaucourt. The British Fifth Army conducted large attacks in October and early November, launching the final set piece battle of the Somme Offensive, the Battle of the Ancre on 13 November.

16GW1073 October 1916: panoramic view of the Ancre Valley, looking left to right towards Beaucourt, Miraumont, St Pierre Divion, the Schwaben Redoubt and Thiepval.

16GW1074 Men of a Highland regiment with a captured German trench mortar, November 1916.

16GW1075 A chain of men passing shells near St Pierre Divion, November 1916.

16GW1077 Captured German equipment, including many stick grenades, St Pierre Divion, November 1916.

16GW1079 As another winter of trench warfare looms, British soldiers took to wearing goat skin overcoats as in the previous winter months.

16GW1076 German barbed wire entanglements near Beaumont Hamel, November 1916.

16GW1080 A light sprinkling of snow heralded the miseries of another winter in the trenches.

16GW1081 Men of the 17th Battalion, London Regiment, passing along the Ancre Valley in the early winter of 1916/17.

16GW1084 British and French soldiers sorting through salvaged German rifles, looking for workable weapons.

16GW772 Moving supplies in deriorating weather conditions made it very heavy work for the horse teams.

16GW1072 This horse is loaded with trench waders.

16GW1082 This mule is being cleaned up after getting stuck in the mud.

16GW1083 The only way to transport artillery shells when the roads can no longer carry vehicles. These mules are carrying ten artillery rounds each..

16GW768 A battalion on the march, with a Company cooker steaming with hot food, ready for when a break is called or the destination reached.

16GW778 Company cooks working to deliver a hot meal.

16GW777 Three British soldiers enjoying hot food during the fighting in the Ancre Valley area in the winter of 1916.

16GW776 British troops eating a meal on Christmas day in a shell hole near Beaumont Hamel on the Somme. Note the close proximity of a grave.

In March 1917, the Germans made a strategic withdrawal up to thirty kilometres east of the Somme front: positions there were hardly favourable and required excessive manpower.The new position became known to the British as the Hindenburg Line.

British troops on the Somme
seen advancing to occupy vacated ground
around the German strongpoint at the
village of Serre.

Information used in this chapter was based on the
following titles in the **Battleground Europe** series
of guide books:

Pozières by Graham Keech
Fricourt-Mametz, *Thiepval* and *La Boisselle*
by Michael Stedman
Mametz Wood by Michael Renshaw
Delville Wood and *Beaumont Hamel*
by Nigel Cave
Courcelette, *Combles* and *Walking the Somme*
by Paul Reed
Flers & Gueudecourt and *Boom Ravine*
by Trevor Pigeon

These are available from
Pen & Sword History Books Ltd.

General Index